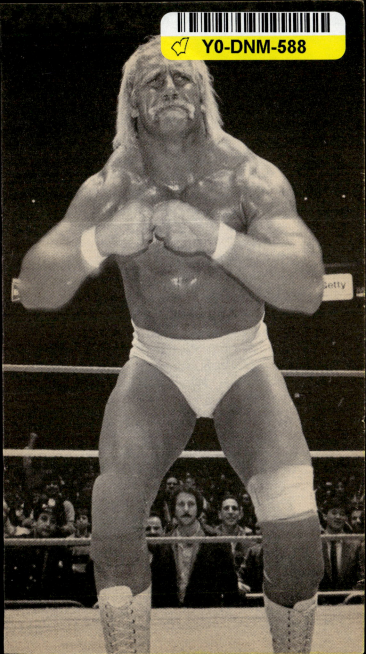

This book is dedicated to three special friends: to Anamaria, for providing the requisite moral support; to Jason Neyland Martin, a future Heisman Trophy winner, for giving me all those smiles; and last but not least to my grandfather, who twenty-five years ago taught me about the wonders of flying dropkicks and Bruno Sammartino.

Acknowledgments

My sincere thanks to Fran Miller, who was kind enough to set aside greed and sell me a ticket to Wrestlemania at face value. In addition, my sincere gratitude to Barbara B., Barbara G., Chris, Deborah, Bill, McKevin, Linda, Diane and, of course, Lonesome Dave.

HULKAMANIA!

HULK HOGAN, AMERICA'S HERO

ABBOT NEIL

PUBLISHED BY POCKET BOOKS NEW YORK

Another *Original* publication of POCKET BOOKS

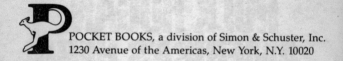

POCKET BOOKS, a division of Simon & Schuster, Inc.
1230 Avenue of the Americas, New York, N.Y. 10020

Produced by Cloverdale Press, Inc. 133 Fifth Ave., NY, NY 10003
Designed by Linda Fiordilino

ISBN: 0-671-60678-6

First Pocket Books printing June, 1985

10 9 8 7 6 5 4 3 2 1

POCKET and colophon are registered trademarks
of Simon & Schuster, Inc.

Printed in the U.S.A.

CONTENTS

Hogan slams a forearm in Rowdy Roddy's back.

Introduction

Nobody does it better. So move over, James Bond—Hulk Hogan's in town, after accomplishing the impossible. The Hulkster took the dwindling industry of professional wrestling and turned it into the media and entertainment event of the decade—HULKAMANIA!

As the World Wrestling Federation heavyweight champion, Hogan has become the most recognizable athlete in America today. With a combination of unforgettable personality and a six-foot-eight-inch, 300-pound body, Hulk Hogan has become *big* box office. His championship matches are regularly seen by over one million viewers, and his popularity has created a whole new merchandising industry to satisfy the fans' cravings for Hulk T-shirts, toys, and posters.

Hogan, a thirty-year-old native of Venice Beach, California, began his professional wrestling career after a turn at bodybuilding that produced his massive physique. Only a few years later, the Hulk defeated the Iron Sheik at New York's Madison Square Garden and became the ninth man to win the heavyweight title in the twenty-year history of the World Wrestling Federation.

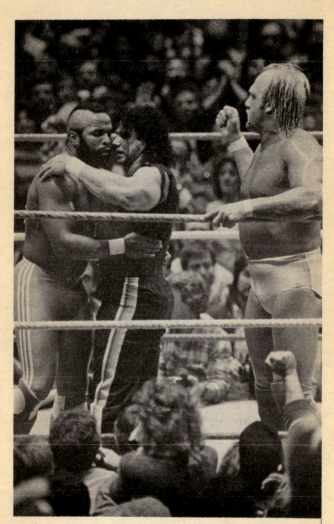

After the Wrestlemania free-for-all, Mr. T aids manager Jimmy ''Superfly'' Snuka as Hulk Hogan keeps an eye out for Piper and Orndorff.

Overseas, Hulk Hogan has developed a following outside the wrestling world. An accomplished bass guitarist, his songs have long been on Japanese music charts. In 1984 his autobiographical song "Itchiban" (translated: "Number One") rose quickly to the top, becoming what the recording industry calls a bullet.

Hogan began hitting the spotlight with his memorable portrayal of Thunderlips in Sylvester Stallone's movie *Rocky III*. Since then the Hulkster has appeared on most of the nation's popular television shows, including Johnny Carson's *Tonight* show and NBC's *Saturday Night Live*.

Just how Hulk Hogan became a media event is the story of *Hulkamania*. But it's more than just a wrestling story: it's about believing in yourself and rising to the top, against all the odds. It's about the triumph of good over evil. It's about patriotism. In fact, the whole concept of Hulkamania represents the ideals created by another famous man of steel—the ideals of truth, justice, and the American way!

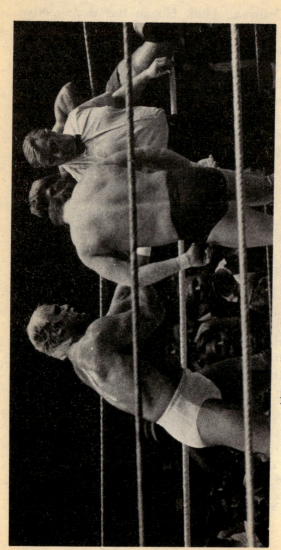

Hogan slams a forearm smash to Rowdy Roddy.

CHAPTER ONE

Welcome to Hulkamania!

You're wearing a T-shirt with the words "American-Made" emblazoned on it. Your son never leaves the house without his trusted Hulk Hogan doll. Lately, you've found yourself walking down the street whistling the tune "Eye of the Tiger."

Upset? Don't worry, sports fans, you've just entered the wrestling–entertainment world of Hulkamania.

Separated by the referee during 1985's main event, Piper and Mr. T stage a staredown, as an anxious Hulkster stalks the ring.

What is Hulkamania?

Just what or who is Hulkamania? It's just the latter-day version of Superman's code of truth, justice, and the American way.

Don't go running to your dictionary just yet. Webster's lacked the foresight to include *Hulkamania* in its latest edition. Rest assured, however, that if the "mania" keeps rolling it's just a matter of time.

Hulkamania is the brainstorm of the modern-day P.T. Barnum, professional wrestling promoter Vince McMahon, Jr. Perhaps the best spokesman for the craze—both Hulkamania and Wrestlemania—is none other than the Hulk, the Hulkster, the new American Hero—Hulk Hogan. In his own words on ABC's 20/20, the Hulk tried to explain Hulkamania. "What's it all about? I'll tell you what Hulkamania is all about. It's indescribable! Brother, you got to live it, you got to experience it. You got to have it flow in your blood before you can even come close to believing in it or comprehending it."

Now that we have heard the gospel straight from the Hulk's mouth, let's find out where Hulkamania came from.

The Hulkster in his "American Made" T-shirt.

The Origins of the Hulk

In the beginning, California created Terry Jean Bollette, a part-time bass guitarist in a typical rock band. Between gigs, Bollette, like many others from Venice Beach — popularly known as Muscle Beach — began pumping iron. Like an ugly caterpillar changing into a beautiful butterfly, Bollette evolved into Hulk Hogan. His six-foot-eight-inch frame quickly filled out to a muscular 320 pounds. His sun-streaked blond hair and deeply tanned body soon made him a big hit with the California girls. Bored with his life-style, Hogan sought out new employment. The first rumblings of Hulkamania were heard in 1976. Ironically, the man who convinced Hogan to try professional wrestling, Freddie Blassie, is known around the world as the manager of the professional bad guys. Villains like the Wild Samoans, the Iron Sheik, and Nikolai Volkoff are all under Blassie's care. The wrestling world is sharply divided into two camps: good guys and bad guys. But Hogan wouldn't last long as a villain.

Hogan began intensive training, under Blassie's supervision. Six months later he was ready for action. To the fans the immediate association with Blassie meant only one thing — the Hulk was evil and must be booed.

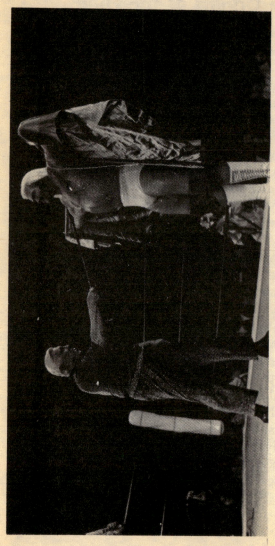

Early in his career, Hogan, managed by Freddie Blassie, displays his well-developed physique.

For Blassie's purpose however, the Hulk presented a problem. Hogan was blond, big, strong, and almost too good-looking to play the villain. In the ring, he was so animated, so charismatic, that even die-hard wrestling fans could hardly work up the desire to hiss and boo. Something had to change.

Rise to Stardom

What happened was a true-life Hollywood fantasy. Sylvester Stallone was looking for an unknown wrestler to play the role of Thunder-lips in *Rocky III*. Hello, Hulk Hogan. Hogan played the wrestler who embarasses Rocky in the ring. A wrestler embarassing a boxer...sound familiar? For all you history buffs, this scene was derived from an actual encounter between Muhammad Ali and the Manchurian Giant, Gorilla Monsoon, in 1974. Monsoon told NBC's *SportsWorld*, "Ali had just signed a match to wrestle the Japanese champion, Anoki. I guess in his own mind he said, let me go down to the arena and see what I got myself into. Well, before I knew it, there was Muhammad, bare chested, taunting me in the ring, taking a few jabs. He was calling me names the whole time. When he got close enough, I just picked him up on my shoulders, gave him a nice airplane ride and slammed him to the mat. He stayed on his back looking stunned. I guess he got a good taste of what professional wrestling was all about."

The exposure Hulk Hogan received from *Rocky III* made him an instant box office star on the wrestling circuit. Predictably, no star in the grappling galaxy eludes Vince McMahon, Jr. McMahon quickly bought up Hogan's contract and made him a regular guest on the World Wrestling Federation's cable show. Hogan became a good guy. His flowing blond hair and Adonis physique were hard to forget. All that was needed was the finishing touch. One night, the Hulk appeared on the broadcast wearing a bright red T-shirt proclaiming on it "American-Made." Hulk Hogan became the next best thing to Mom and apple pie.

The Main Event

Using the movie and television exposure, McMahon ushered Hogan to New York's mecca of professional wrestling, Madison Square Garden. One month later, the capacity crowd was treated to the main event: The WWF Champion, the Iron Sheik, against America's Hero, Hulk Hogan.

The crowd began to roar as they heard the

theme from *Rocky III*, "Eye of the Tiger." Rising to their feet, they greeted Hulk Hogan as he rushed to the ring. Wearing his now-famous "American-Made" T-shirt, the Hulk confronted the champion. What took place was the classic confrontation between good and evil. The Sheik, from Tehran, entered the ring with an Iranian flag draped over his head. For the Garden fans it was more than Hulk Hogan against the Iron Sheik. This was the American way against the evils of the Ayatollah.

The action was fast and furious. Hogan missed a flying body block and smacked into the turnbuckle. Hogan crashed to the mat, stunned from the blow. Seizing the ripe opportunity to finish off his challenger, the Iron Sheik turned Hogan on his stomach, reached under his arms, and locked his Middle Eastern hands around the Great White Hope's chin. Now leaning on Hogan's back and pulling on his chin, the Sheik applied his famous Camel Clutch. The fans went wild trying to help their hero, because everyone knew nobody had ever gotten out of the Camel Clutch.

Maybe it was the collective will of the crowd, but just when all seemed lost, the Hulk began to stir. Still in the Clutch, Hogan worked his way to one knee. The crowd, sensing wrestling history, went wild as the Hulk slowly rose

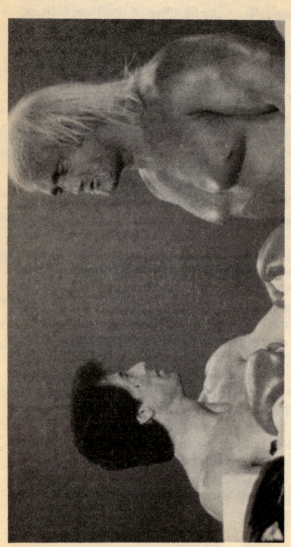

Sylvester Stalone as Rocky Balboa stares in amazement at "Thunderlips," played by Hulk Hogan in *Rocky III*.

to his feet. The Sheik was so shocked that all he could do was hold on to Hogan's back. Glancing at the crazed crowd for moral support, Hogan drove the Sheik backwards into the turnbuckle. The stunned Sheik dropped off Hogan's back in obvious pain. Hogan, as if possessed, bounced off the ropes and drove his elbow into the thick neck of the Iron Sheik. The Sheik dropped to the mat, and after the referee counted him out, the World Wrestling Federation had a new champion — Hulk Hogan.

The crowd was then treated to Hogan's version of Hulkamania. As "Eye of the Tiger" boomed over the crowd, the Hulk, now wearing his championship belt, went into his victory dance of bodybuilding poses. The crowd began taking up the chant of "U.S.A.! U.S.A.!" America had beaten Iran. Hulk Hogan was the new champion. And beyond any shadow of a doubt — Hulkamania was born.

In the Words of the Hulk...

Now that you know a little bit about how Hulkamania happened, let's hear another version from Hogan himself. This time the interviewer is Bob Costas for NBC's *SportsWorld*. "What is Hulkamania? I tell you something, Bashful Bob, you must have been out in a log

Hulk Hogan straps on the World Wrestling Federation championship belt after defeating the Iron Sheik.

cabin somewhere, with no television, no indoor plumbing, no electricity, no newspapers. First thing, Hulkamania is about getting your act together. Getting rid of those puny chicken-wing arms. Getting into the gym for some heavy-duty weight and conditioning training. But along with that you have to say your prayers and eat your vitamins…But as far as Hulkamania is concerned, you've got to get all that done first, before you can be in my club, brother. Hulkamania is like a fever, man. It's like the plague, but a good plague. Everywhere you go, everything you do has got to be positive, man! Everything I do is real, and my people get off on that. I live this thing day and night. It's me. It's my ability to drive others to make something out of their lives. It's rampant Hulkamania!"

Perhaps Hulkamania cannot be defined. Maybe it only exists in the collective mind of Hogan enthusiasts who seemingly live and die with each of their hero's exploits.

Hulk Hogan raises his championship belt before a capacity crowd in Japan.

★ ★ ★ ★ ★ CHAPTER TWO ★ ★ ★ ★ ★

Before the Hulk

If Hulk Hogan had been born 2,000 years ago, he probably would have packed the Parthenon instead of Madison Square Garden. Unlike other popular sports such as basketball and football that evolved only over the past several decades, wrestling can trace its origins to ancient Egypt and Greece.

Every young creature engages in some sort of wrestling. Puppies and children are always "mixing it up" in a playful game of wrestling. Modern-day professional wrestling probably originated from this basic nonviolent combat.

Rules of the Game

Researching the sport yields evidence of the formation of rules governing legal holds and moves. By providing a way to determine the winner these Greek and Egyptian innovators of the sport limited the length of each contest. To be victorious, the winner had to "pin" his opponent's shoulders to the mat.

Today there are two sets of rules – the strictly formulated set of collegiate rules and the looser, free-for-all style of professional wrestling. For example, in the college ranks a pin is accomplished when the opponent's shoulder touches the mat for only a second. In the razzle-dazzle world of professional wrestling, getting the referee to declare a pin is a long, theatrical process. The professional "rules" call for the opponent's shoulders to touch the canvas for a three-second count. Rarely, if ever, does a pin occur on the first attempt. Despite the foe's fatigue or injuries, that first attempt at a pin is usually thwarted by a bicycle pedaling of the legs that magically tosses the would-be winner off the escaping wrestler.

The Big Time

Novice fans of professional wrestling may go to an arena expecting to see the familiar Olympic style complete with the standard takedowns and reversals. The shock sets in when the ring announcer proclaims a "one fall, one-hour time limit." Accustomed to the college style of eight-minute matches, the novice professional wrestling fan wearily starts to settle in for a long afternoon of hour-long bouts. Soon the fan's anguish disappears as he witnesses for the first time the fast-paced world of Hulk Hogan and his brethren. Professional wrestling is hard-hitting excitement. Matches are won by pins, disqualifications, or submissions!

To highlight the differences between the amateurs and the pros, consider a few of the generally regarded rules of sportsmanship so common to the collegiate style and so foreign to professional wrestling. The college rules of sportsmanship include: never try to punish an opponent; never lose your temper; be courteous to opponents and officials; and be gracious in winning or losing. Watch any professional match and you'll soon see that to survive, a wrestler must toss out these rules and fight for his life.

Professional wrestling as practiced by masters such as Hulk Hogan seems to have an almost "anything goes" set of rules. The concept of sportsmanship, so common in the collegiate field, is rarely seen during a professional wrestling match. This is not to say that professional

Under the watchful eye of Freddie "Ayatollah" Blassie, Nikolai Volkoff sings the Russian National Anthem at Madison Square Garden.

wrestling lacks its fair share of gentleman athletes. On the contrary, the professional wrestlers are easily grouped into two categories: good guys and bad guys.

Good Guys vs. Bad Guys

Most wrestling magazines contain a rating system based on popularity. Always included in the most popular good guy category are professionals like Hulk Hogan, Sgt. Slaughter, Andre the Giant, and the Junkyard Dog. On the negative side, in the notorious most-hated column, can be found such villains as Big John Studd, the Iron Sheik, Nikolai Volkoff, and of course, Rowdy Roddy Piper.

The good-guy bad-guy split exists because professional wrestling is both a sport and entertainment. In this world of big-money bouts, wrestling promoters stir enthusiasm by matching the good guys against the bad guys. Nothing gets a crowd going like seeing Mr. Made-in-America, Hulk Hogan, dethrone the likes of the Iron Sheik to gain the World Wrestling Federation Championship Belt.

Wrestling Through the Ages

The sport of wrestling goes back to the dawn of recorded time. The ancient Sumerians were working on their takedowns some 5,000 years before the birth of Christ. King Henry VIII of England was a noted wrestling fan. Even young Abe Lincoln got into the act. In the town of New Salem, Illinois, the famed rail splitter acquired quite a reputation as a grappler. One recorded confrontation took place between Lincoln and a guy named, of all things, Jack Armstrong. Lincoln won the match and collected his $10 prize. As Lincoln biographer Carl Sandburg related, "Lincoln picked him up by the neck and waved him around like a rag. Then as the small crowd gasped, he threw him down to a hard fall." If Lincoln were still wrestling today, he would, no doubt, be a popular member of Vince McMahon's World Wrestling Federation, probably billed as "Honest Abe."

In the 1930s, a wrestler had appeared on the scene who gave new meaning to the term "heavyweight." This 400-pound Goliath aptly wrestled under the name Man Mountain Dean. Many credit Dean with inventing the Crusher. For Dean it was a very effective hold. After all, how many men could survive 400 pounds of muscle pinning them to the mat?

The girth made so popular by Man Mountain Dean prompted other "nonsvelte" wrestlers to enter the sport later on. Wrestlers such as Haystack Calhoun and Gorilla Monsoon rose to power some twenty years later.

Heroes of the 1950s

Modern-day heroes such as Hulk Hogan can trace their contemporary origins back to the 1950s. During the Eisenhower Administration, professional wrestling became a mainstay on the baby of the communications industry — television. Weekly, millions of Americans were glued to their tiny, brand new televisions watching their newfound heroes such as Gorgeous George and Bruno Sammartino. The overly blond Gorgeous George would captivate the live crowd by presenting flowers to the ladies and dousing himself with cologne.

It was Gorgeous George who first gave wrestling a national following and a degree of dignity. Bud Collins of NBC's *SportsWorld* said, "He had the heart of a roughneck, but the soul of the poet. Women found his perfumed body a welcome change from the sweat dripping from most wrestlers." George spent hours getting groomed before a match. He might put his thumb in his foe's eye, but at least it wasn't dirty or unmanicured. Later, the Gorgeous George image would be caricatured by the actor Henry Winkler in the film *The One and Only*.

Gorgeous George continued to be a wrestling legend well into the 1950s. After the Second World War, televised wrestling became an American mainstay. In fact, the comedian

Two of yesteryear's superstars, Bruno Sammartino and a barefooted Antonino Rocca, battle it out at Madison Square Garden.

Steve Allen served as an announcer on some early bouts. He remembers, "Gorgeous George was the first to wear long hair. He preceded the hippies by twenty-five years. Back in 1945, men just didn't wear long hair, but I guess if you're 300 pounds, you can wear any kind of hair you want."

The 1950s brought two new stars and new techniques to the wrestling world. Antonino Rocca became well known for his acrobatics in the ring. Rocca would surprise his opponents by leaping and cartwheeling around the canvas. More often than not, Rocca ended his matches by flying feet-first and locking his powerful legs around an opponent's neck.

Later in that same decade came Killer Kowalski. Unlike Antonino Rocca, Kowalski relied on his powerful hands. He'd wrap them around an opponent's neck, manipulating them into his famous Claw Hold.

Bruno Sammartino

The first superstar of the 1960s had to be the immortal Bruno Sammartino. Unlike the Gorgeous George types, whose stock in trade was gimmicks, Sammartino relied on his strength and gentlemanly manner to crush his opponents and sway the fans. Bruno held the title for

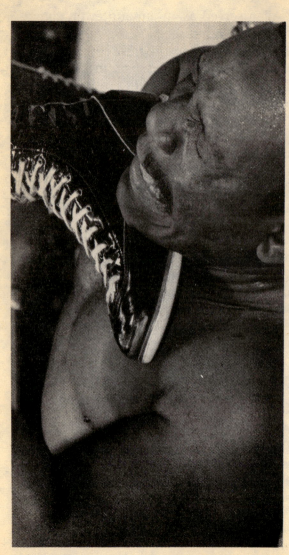

Special Delivery Jones grimaces as Brutus Beefcake applies his polished boot to the throat.

so long that many of today's fans still refer to him as the champ.

According to Sammartino contemporary Gorilla Monsoon, "Bruno was the greatest to ever hold the championship belt. He did it for over fifteen years and I'm sure no man will ever do that again. I remember one time at Madison Square Garden," he told NBC's Bud Collins, "he was fighting Stan Hanson. Early in the bout, Hanson whipped Sammartino against the corner turnbuckle. Bruno's head snapped back. His neck was broken! Bruno told me later it hurt badly, but he didn't know it was broken. Bruno was so strong that he came back a few minutes later and beat Hanson to successfully defend his title."

Bruno was the Muhammad Ali of wrestling; and despite his present age, he remains the crowd favorite. One need only examine a small piece of Wrestlemania during the March 31, 1985 bout at Madison Square Garden to establish this fact. Bruno served as the corner man during the match between his son, David, and the evil Brutus Beefcake, who according to the ring announcer, "hails from points unknown." Soon after the opening bell the match got out of hand. Beefcake threw David Sammartino out of the ring and proceeded to beat him with a metal folding chair. As the Madison

Square Garden capacity crowd began chanting, "Bruno, Bruno, Bruno..." the elder Sammartino chased Brutus Beefcake back into the ring. What followed seemed to be a flashback to Bruno's early years as America's favorite wrestler. With the Garden fans in a frenzy, Bruno drop-kicked the stunned Beefcake out of the ring. Acknowledging the roar of the crowd, Bruno waved good-bye to his fans and, arm around his son, left the ring.

The Bad Guys

As long as we're discussing wrestling history, let's talk about the ancestral roots that yielded such bad guys as the Iron Sheik and Nikolai Volkoff. Just as these contemporary villains are associated with America's enemies Iran and Russia, so the old-time bad guys were linked to some of our country's older rivals. Hailed as "the greatest oriental master of all time," Professor Toru Tanaka began his career as one of Bruno's last rivals. As he told *Ringside*, "My matches against Bruno Sammartino were the toughest battles I've ever had. We had all kinds of battles, and the fans will never forget them." Ironically, some twenty years later, Tanaka has come out of retirement to wrestle Bruno's son, David.

The Sammartino family bridges the gap between the early 1960s and present-day wrestlers. Professor Tanaka comments, "It's funny, now I'm wrestling his son. I just wrestled him [David] several years ago in Puerto Rico. At the time he was new and just learning the sport. Today he has several years under his belt and he needs the experience when he steps into the ring to face me. I will say that boy is making it on his own. He doesn't rely on his daddy's reputation."

The Sammartino-Tanaka matches have even withstood the test of time. Today's hero, David Sammartino, can still recall one of his father's bouts with the Japanese professor. As he told Gregory Joseph, "Out of all my dad's opponents, Professor Tanaka sticks out most in my mind. I remember when I was a little kid and I saw Tanaka bloody up my father real bad. I was mad. I hurt and to this day I've never forgotten it. I've got a score to settle with him and no matter how long it takes I will knock away that nightmare."

The Crazies

Another segment of Hulk Hogan's foes can best be categorized as "the crazies." These individuals, such as George "The Animal" Steele, seem at times to be uncontrollably mad. According to referee Al Vass, "I've been in the ring with that man many times, and I've never seen a crazier wrestler. I never know if he even understands me when I tell him to break a hold: he just looks at you with those rolling eyes and starts grunting and groaning like a rhinoceros. Refereeing a George Steele match is like being trapped in a cage with a rabid Saint Bernard."

An odd combination of good looks and crazy behavior, "Crazy" Luke Graham thrilled wrestling audiences in the early 1960s. As Graham approached the ring apron, the crowd would whip him into a frenzy with chants of "Crazy Luke...Crazy Luke." Once in the ring, Graham would smack himself on the side of his head to stop what he insisted was the sound of bells. This madness continued throughout the bout, serving to confuse his opponents and entertain the fans.

The Decline in the 1960s

Sometime during the 1960s professional wrestling lost its popularity. Overexposure, the preoccupation with the war in Vietnam, and the rise of "legitimate" sports such as the National Football League teams have all been used to explain the decline of professional wrestling.

Wrestling dropped out of the main arenas

in the country. A hard-core group of promoters began selling their product to smaller theaters and high school gymnasiums. The once-unified wrestling world broke down into regional championships, many of which still exist today. To save money, promoters such as St. Louis's Sam Muchnick and Vince McMahon, Sr., set up wrestling confederations localized throughout the country. Today, despite the obvious popularity and dominance of the World Wrestling Federation and its heavyweight champion Hulk Hogan, many other wrestling associations still remain. Some of these are the Mid-Atlantic, Mid-South, Georgia, Northwest, World Class, and Florida associations. In the Hawaiian Islands, the Polynesian Pacific Association rules the wrestling roost.

As wrestling's popularity declined during the 1960s, wrestling promoters began hyping their programs with gimmicks. Their major attempt to draw big crowds centered on staged grudge matches. Six- and sometimes eight-man tag-team matches would often end up with all the combatants slugging it out in the middle of the ring. Steel-cage bouts sprung up where two gladiators were locked up with "no escape for the loser." Throughout the land desperate promoters tried to draw in customers with lumberjack contests, street fights between wrestlers, and of course masked men and midgets. Wrestling was clearly on the decline.

Vince McMahon, Jr., and the 1980s

So what happened? What happened is that Vince McMahon, Sr., sired a son, Vince McMahon, Jr. Vince junior took the floundering wrestling world by storm and within three years created the hottest entertainment property of the 1980s. Vince McMahon, Jr., took the same basic plan of good guy–bad guy and engineered the wrestling revival. As McMahon told *Newsweek*, "The same basic formulas have worked pretty well for the last fifty years." Thanks to the ministrations of McMahon, the World Wrestling Federation (WWF) is now one of the world's most famous traveling road shows. Starting from a power base in the Northwest, the WWF now promotes four shows a night nationwide as well as those held in foreign sites such as Japan and the Middle East. The monthly card at Madison Square Garden in New York regularly sells out the 24,000-seat arena. The bouts have become so popular that they have been simulcast nationwide on closed-circuit television.

Vince McMahon, Jr., the man who saved professional wrestling.

McMahon noticed that the 1980s brought on such fringe entertainment as bodybuilding and the various battles of the network stars. Professional wrestling was only a hop, skip, and a body slam away. The other factor that helped McMahon promote his WWF was the increase in the number of American households with cable TV. Now that he had the potential to attract an audience, all that was missing was a strategy designed to lure and keep the crowd. Little did McMahon realize that his strategy was being inadvertently mapped out by the new female sensation in rock 'n' roll, Cyndi Lauper. Thanks to the blending of wrestling and rock 'n' roll, televised wrestling of the WWF soon had four programs in the top ten of cable shows.

The high ratings are certainly satisfying for McMahon, but more surprising is the audience behind the ratings. Despite the common belief that the typical wrestling fan is a middle-aged man sitting before his television gulping down a beer, the demographics show otherwise. According to the industry rating source, *Advertising Age*, 40 percent of the people watching the Hulk defend his WWF crown are women. And, more than half these viewers are between eighteen and forty-five years old. Wrestling, like its newly adopted family, rock 'n' roll, is here to stay.

Mr. In-Vince-Able

Vince McMahon, Jr., is living proof that genetics really work. Vince junior inherited his gift of recognizing wrestling talent from the master of the game, his father, Vince McMahon, Sr.

And, in a blending of generations, one of Vince senior's last wrestling discoveries is presently one of Vince junior's mainstays. Vince senior traveled to Quebec during the early 1970s to see a wrestler one struggling promoter referred to as "one big dude." Wrestling was foundering, and Vince senior thought that perhaps this "big dude" would help. Vince senior met Andre the Giant. As he told *Sports Illustrated*, "My initial thought was, 'My God, I never saw such a man!' I'd seen photographs and videotapes, of course, and I knew Andre was seven feet four inches and over 400 pounds, but I simply wasn't prepared for how he looked up close. He was unlike anything I'd ever seen before, and I knew he could become the number one draw in wrestling."

The Giant from the North

Like a true showman, Vince senior realized that two changes had to be made to promote the Giant and transform him into a wrestling superstar. For openers, the Giant was wrestling with the name Jean Ferré to please the French Canadian fans. Second, he was wrestling every week in the same arena. Vince senior convinced the big man to use the sobriquet "Andre the Giant." The elder McMahon correctly realized that the straightforward naming approach was sufficient. Wrestling had become inundated with names like the Masked Avenger, the Butcher, Gorilla Monsoon, and so forth. Andre the Giant...here was an immediately recognizable name just waiting to roll off the American tongue.

Now that Vince senior was molding a potential superstar, the problem became how to handle the bookings. He explained his method to *Sports Illustrated*. "I saw right away that Andre needed to be booked into a place no more than a few times a year. Most of our wrestlers work one of our circuits for a while and then move to another. It keeps things fresh. A guy may work New England for a few months...go from there to the South and then on out to spend some time in Minneapolis."

Vince senior's method of promoting Andre the Giant changed the wrestling world. Studying that promotion served as part of Vince junior's education. According to Vince senior, "Andre's different. The whole world is his cir-

Andre the Giant has his hands full.

cuit. By making his visits few and far between he never becomes commonplace. Now, wherever he goes, the gates are larger than they would be without him. I book him for three visits a year to Japan, two to Australia, two to Europe, and the rest of the time I book him into the major arenas of the United States."

Obviously, this new formula of limited bookings proved successful. People, anxious to be among the select few to see the Giant, packed the arenas. Concludes McMahon, "The wrestlers and promoters all want him on their cards, because when the Giant comes, everyone makes more money."

The Mountain and the Mousse

Another lesson to be learned from the elder McMahon was a crash course in creating a likeable image. Vince senior's plan was simply brilliant. Despite Andre's huge size, he was actually a gentle person. Now it's no secret that Andre the Giant consumes huge quantities of food. But, Andre was no franks-and-beans advocate. Vince senior soon learned that the Giant was a gourmand. As related by the *Sports Illustrated* reporter, "...As he globe-hops, the Giant usually avoids this kind of unpleasantness by exercising great care in his choice of restaurants.

He takes the same sort of delight Hemingway did in scheduling his travel arrangements so as to arrive at the time and place that will allow him a chance to have a word with the owner and local friends and sample the specialty of the house. Although he admits to a slight preference for French cuisine, he introduced me to a Korean restaurant in Manhattan, a delicatessen in Montreal and an Italian place in Albany …But the spot he seemed most pleased to show me was, understandably, a delightful Montreal restaurant, Le Picher, which he owns."

Suddenly, Andre the Giant began appearing on nationwide television talk shows. It was hard for America to forget the image of this towering, seven-foot-four-inch man preparing a salmon mousse.

In His Father's Footsteps

What the young McMahon, Vince junior, learned from all this has catapulted him into being America's foremost wrestling promoter. At thirty-nine Vince junior is not only a product of his legendary father, but as a baby-boomer, he has learned about the power of television and rock music. How did he turn this experience into a multimillion dollar business?

The Vince McMahon, Jr., story reads like a Hollywood script. Learning the trade from his father, Vince junior went on to create the biggest phenomenon in the history of wrestling – Hulkamania!

Like many boys, Vince junior was so caught up in his father's success that he wanted in on the business. His first ambition wasn't to be a promoter, though. He wanted to wrestle. Vince senior put a fast end to this dream, but Vince junior continued to lift weights and exercise. So once he acquired his muscular physique, McMahon junior, unable to convince his father to let him in the ring, turned to promoting... not wrestling, but rock 'n' roll!

The Rock-Wrestling Connection

The Vince McMahon, Jr., empire got its first promotional baptism in 1979. Vince junior bought the small Cape Cod Arena in Yarmouth, Massachusetts. He converted an old hockey arena into a rock 'n' roll theater that catered to the Cape's summertime throngs. As Vince junior watched rock groups like The Clash and Elvis Costello come and go he soon recognized the amazing link between rock music performers and his first love, wrestling. Certain rock groups, like particular wrestlers, relied on pure musical talent to captivate the audience. People flocked to see Van Morrison, as they had once come to see Bruno Sammartino.

The genius of Vince McMahon, Jr., surfaced when he realized that there were other rock groups who relied more on outlandish theatrical productions than on musical ability to drive audiences into a frenzy. Rock fans went wild over the band Kiss, with their heavy makeup and staged productions. In like fashion, wrestling fans loved to scream and shout at the crazy antics of grapplers like Abdullah the Butcher. Vince junior soon formulated a plan to promote wrestling as pure fan entertainment, despite any questions of authenticity. As he told *The Los Angeles Times*, "The old-timers [fans] attempt to build in credibility based on ring performance alone. It really doesn't matter to me whether someone believes it's real or fake. It matters that they enjoy what we do, the performance inside and outside the ring."

Waiting in the Wings

While Vince junior was formulating his theory of wrestling promotion, somewhere in Venice, California, a man aptly named Hulk Hogan was busy pumping iron, getting a tan, and breaking girls' hearts.

Vince junior was still a few years away from developing Hogan into America's favorite matinee idol. McMahon was busy creating a surefire formula to capture the hearts and minds of the people. His father's basic philosophy was too closely aligned with formalized ranking procedures like those found in boxing. Wrestlers were still using old tricks to keep the crowd's attention. They appeared almost exclusively in the ring. Off the mat, few wrestlers gained any recognition. Vince senior's method involved increasing a wrestler's "work rate." In the lingo of the wrestling world, work rate refers to the number of lumps, bumps, and body slams a wrestler puts up with during a match. The elder McMahon's philosophy hinged on the principle that the greater the work rate, the greater the popularity of the wrestler.

Vince McMahon, Jr., had a different vision regarding the wrestling world. As he told NBC's Bob Costas, "Early on, I decided to make a combination of wrestling as a sport and show business my number one priority."

The Rise of the WWF

Vince started developing the World Wrestling Federation with an idealistic attitude. "The goal of the World Wrestling Federation is to be the very best at everything we do. I want to promote the best cards, the best events, the best toys and cartoons. Our network, cable broadcasts, and closed-circuit events must be untouchable."

After the death of the elder McMahon in 1982, Vince embarked on his campaign to promote professional wrestling and the World Wrestling Federation as "the premiere source of sports entertainment." After just three years at the helm, his success has been staggering.

Before Vince junior took control of the WWF, any mention of wrestling would make people laugh as if they were hearing a bad joke. Today, professional wrestling is anything but a funny business. Take a look at the cable ratings of sports events. The cable broadcasts put together by McMahon's WWF have pinned back the ears of college football and basketball by as much as three to one.

The other numbers are staggering, too. NBC's *SportsWorld* estimated that, thanks in large part to McMahon's promotion, professional wrestling has become a $250,000,000 a year business. Ten million people a year push their way through the turnstiles to see live events. Including the various televised programs, an estimated 25,000,000 people view wrestling each year.

The World Wrestling Federation of Vince

Hulkamaniacs cheer as Hogan and Mr. T enter the ring at the event of 1985—Wrestlemania.

McMahon has about 300 wrestling cards a year. Crowd favorites such as Hulk Hogan can now wrestle all over the country as often as six times a week. Thanks to Vince junior, Hulkamania has made professional wrestling a powerhouse in sports entertainment.

In Vince's own words on ABC's *20/20,* "The sport of professional wrestling is growing by leaps and bounds. In terms of popularity it's almost overwhelming. By far, I'm the biggest promoter and I work hard to maintain and enjoy that privilege."

The Fans

Just who are these people who get whipped into a frenzy as Hulk Hogan approaches the ring? According to University of Maryland professor Larry Mintz, "The fans of professional wrestling fall into many categories. There's a group who really get into the violence and want to see people hurt. They believe it. They love to stomp their feet and yell and scream. Then there's a second group who view it as theater. They are willing to suspend their disbelief. To them it's like watching *The A Team.*"

No matter why people attend professional wrestling events, there can be no denying that once you've witnessed the phenomenon, it's hard to forget the excitement. Even the biggest skeptics soon find themselves caught up in the groundswell as they cheer for heroes like Hulk Hogan to destroy the bad guys like the Iron Sheik.

Bring Back the Heroes

McMahon created Hulkamania but he didn't stop there. Having paved the way for the Hulk's rise to glory, McMahon turned his attention to promoting the entire sport. Realizing that patriotism was again in vogue, McMahon capitalized on "a former member of the Marine Corps," Sgt. Slaughter. As Slaughter enters the ring, dressed in full fatigues, he hands out little American flags. Once inside, Sgt. Slaughter leads the crowd in a stirring rendition of "The Battle Hymn of the Republic."

Playing off the patriotism angle, McMahon pitted Slaughter against two opponents who symbolized America's enemies, the Iron Sheik from Iran and Nikolai Volkoff from Russia. As Volkoff begins to sing the Russion national anthem, somewhere in America McMahon is smiling as thousands of fans hurl debris at the Moscow Menace.

It took Vince McMahon, Jr., to fully realize the potential of exposing the good and evil sides of life. America was frustrated by the hostage situation in Iran, but we could cheer Sgt. Slaughter as he thumped the Teheran Terror, the Iron Sheik. Like the morality plays of ancient England or the tragedies of Greece, wrestling, thanks to McMahon, presented a well-defined struggle between good and evil.

Although 65 percent of wrestling fans are at least high school educated, one doesn't need a diploma to tell the good guys from the bad guys. As Mean Gene Okerlund, a famous ring announcer, said, "It's easy entertainment for people. They like to come sit down at a professional wrestling event and be entertained. Pure and simple. Here you can watch in clear terms the triumph of good over evil. Here your belief that hard work and good moral judgment lead to victory is reinforced. It's all just as easy on the head."

On ABC just prior to his tag-team match with Hulk Hogan, Mr. T summed up his feelings about wrestling's appeal. "Here it's cut and dry. You have a bad guy and a good guy. So the people come to watch, and exhaust their anger. People today are angry for lots of reasons. A lot of people hate their work, their boss. Here at a professional wrestling event they can take it out on the bad guy. They can come in here and relieve their tension."

NBC's sportscaster, Bob Costas (center) is surrounded by superstars (left to right) Mike Rotundo, Hillbilly Jim, Hulk Hogan and Barry Windham.

TNT

Having captivated the big arenas, McMahon turned his attention to the vast number of television viewers. He initiated a show called *Tuesday Night Titans* or *TNT*. *TNT* became such an instant hit that USA cable moved it to Friday night. *TNT* remains the perfect format for promoting professional wrestling. Every week, the tuxedoed McMahon and his trusty sidekick, Lord Alfred Hays, introduce the wonderkids of professional wrestling in this one-hour talk show format. No longer do wrestlers have to rely on their work rate to achieve reknown.

McMahon brings wrestlers out of the ring, exposing them as heroes or villains we all can relate to. *TNT* has included such segments as Sgt. Slaughter putting his Cobra Corps fan club through drills under the hot South Carolina sun; the wedding of Paul "The Butcher" Vachan, attended by such popular wrestling figures as Captain Lou Albano, Freddie Blassie, and of course everybody's dream team, the Wild Samoans. Speaking of the Wild Samoans, on a *TNT* program, they demonstrated their recipe for their secret strength — a diet of raw fish heads. Now that's entertainment!

The Sky's the Limit

Thanks to the talents of Vince McMahon, Jr., professional wrestling is enjoying its greatest popularity. Plans are in the works for a Saturday morning cartoon show featuring the WWF's superheroes like Hulk Hogan against the bad guys like the Iron Sheik and Nikolai Volkoff. Following in the footsteps of Hollywood's elite, a "Hulkamania" poster featuring a variety of poses has become a hot seller nationwide. Hogan's now famous "American-Made" T-shirts are adorning the backs of fans from Albany to Abilene.

Christmas will bring to the stores dolls modeled after the likes of Hulk Hogan and Big John Studd. Kids all over the world will be spending Christmas day recreating their own version of the famous Chain Fence Challenge.

Sgt. Slaughter has entered the marketing world by offering giant foam-rubber cobras and dog tags for the full-fledged members of his Cobra Corps.

Vince doesn't care what people say, professional wrestling is here to stay.

The Stars Come Out at Night

In a country that has as many celebrities as stars in the Milky Way, it's often difficult for gossip columnists to keep up with all of them. But luckily for the columnists, many of these celebrities are presently congregating in large arenas.

The celebrities are not massing for some grand Hollywood opening night. They are coming out of hiding to cheer for Hulk Hogan and his wrestling contemporaries. Hard to believe? Just listen to Oscar winner Diane Keaton speaking to David Letterman on his national *Late Night* show. "Yes, I was at Madison Square Garden the other night. It was fantastic! I can't believe you've never been to one. I mean once you go, it's hard not to get caught up in all the enthusiasm. I was on my feet screaming and yelling along with the sold-out crowd. The place was packed. It's just so entertaining."

Diane Keaton is not alone in her newfound interest. Recent exhibitions of professional wrestling have attracted such luminaries as Dick Clark, Tina Turner, comedian Joe Piscopo, Danny De Vito, and film director Brian DePalma.

Peter Newman, film and theater producer, has been a fan of wrestling for over twenty years. He told Susan Mulcahy of *The New York Post*, "You come here and it's an excited capacity crowd. You never see crowds like this at a Ranger or a Knicks game. This is the most exciting event I've ever been to."

Pop film maker Andy Warhol is another big

fan. He sits ringside, cheering on all his favorites like the Hulkster. "I met all the guys backstage. I just fell in love with all of them," he told the *Post*. "This is real show biz."

Warhol, also known as one of the world's foremost photographers, always brings his camera. "Sitting in front, I get some great pictures. It's hip, it's exciting. It's America. The acrobatics are unbelievable. The audience is very knowledgeable and incredibly enthusiastic. I think I'll become a regular."

So you don't have to fly to Hollywood to mingle with your favorite celebrities. Just put on your Hulkamania T-shirt, hop into your limo, and boogie on down to your nearby wrestling emporium!

★★★★★CHAPTER THREE★★★★★

Hogan Heroics

The Battles with Big John Studd

Joe Louis had Max Schmeling. Muhammed Ali had Joe Frazier. Hulk Hogan had Big John Studd.

That's Big John Studd. That's "Big" as in six feet ten inches tall. That's "Studd" as in 360 pounds. Big John tried twice to take the World Wrestling Federation Championship Belt away from Hulk Hogan. He came close the first time and was annihilated when he dared to try it again.

The First Match

The first match took place at Madison Square Garden in September of 1984. Hogan was totally unprepared to face Big John. He had been told that his opponent would be Jesse Ventura, another ring villain. But Bobby "The Brain" Heenan, Big John Studd's manager, had other plans. Any wrestling manager knows that the biggest money comes from winning the championship belt. So with plenty of behind-the-scenes machinations, Heenan surprised Hogan by making him face an overly eager Big John Studd. In the book, *The Pictorial History of Wrestling*, Big John boasts, "I am the biggest, meanest, baddest man in the sport!" Speaking about Hulk Hogan, he said, "He can run but he cannot hide. And when I catch him, he'll wish he could hide for the rest of his life, 'cause after I get through with him, he's not going to want to show his face anywhere."

So much for the talk. In their first match, Big John backed up his words with some of the bloodiest action ever to be seen in the ring. Even before the opening bell, the crowd sensed that Hogan was in for a battle. The two grapplers taunted each other, and Hogan, tearing off his own "American-Made" T-shirt, stuck his finger in Studd's face. Big John laughed this off as he waved off Hogan.

Defeated but Still Champion

Once the match got started, the crowd roared in appreciation of the backbreakers and punches thrown by both opponents. Just when it seemed that Hogan was going to take charge, Big John slipped a Sleeper Hold on the champ. Trying to urge the Hulk on, the crowd took up the chant, "Hogan...Hogan." As he had previously survived the Iron Sheik's Camel Clutch, Hogan miraculously survived the Sleeper. But because he was thoroughly weakened by the hold, Big John Studd was able to pick him up and fling him out of the ring. The battered, bleeding Hulk was counted out for not being able to return to the ring. A new champion? Not quite. In professional wrestling, a title can only change hands on a pin. So while many of Hulk Hogan's fans wept or sat stunned in their seats, the Hulk staggered back to his dressing room, defeated but still champion.

Like any true champion, Hogan rarely refuses a challenge.

The Return Match

When Big John Studd demanded a return match, the Hulk was only too happy to oblige. After all, Hogan craved revenge. It's embarrassing for the World Wrestling Federation Champion to be counted out of the ring.

Big John Studd points to the $15,000 body-slam prize held by his manager.

As an added incentive, Big John offered the Hulk $15,000 if Hogan could slam Studd during the match.

At the start of the bout, both grapplers locked up in arm holds, tossing each other around the ring. Hulk Hogan attempted to gain the $15,000 prize money as he tried to position himself to slam Studd. Studd pushed off Hogan and resisted the slam attempt.

Studd then attempted to slam Hogan, but the Hulk pushed him off. As Studd retreated, Hogan charged and made another slam attempt. Studd retaliated by beating Hogan with his fists. A stunned Hogan was thrown against the ropes. The crowd grew silent as Studd drew back a karate chop, waiting for Hogan to rebound off the ropes. All thoughts drifted back to their first meeting when Hogan had taken such a beating. Somehow, the overanxious Studd missed the karate chop. As the crowd roared, Hogan attacked Studd with a series of arm chops topped off with a kick in the head.

With the crowd chanting, "Slam...slam... slam," Hogan shook his head approvingly, grabbed Studd, and attempted a slam. This was a big error. Studd drove his fists into the Hulk's head, sending him sprawling on the canvas.

Again the crowd grew silent as Hulk Hogan staggered to his feet. Big John grabbed Hogan and flung him into the ropes. But then something woke up in the Hulk, because he charged off the ropes and threw his right arm around the neck of an astonished Big John Studd. Hogan followed up the clothesline with some smacks to the head.

Smelling the $15,000 for the slam, Hogan went to grab Studd, but Big John slipped between the ropes and out of the ring. Hogan lunged and hit his head on the announcer's table. Bleeding heavily, he tried to get back into the ring. Studd, sensing that the Hulk was in trouble, grabbed the Champ's head and smacked it against the metal railing on the corner of the ring.

Hogan's blood nearly wiped out his vision as Big John continued to hit him in the head. Desperately, Hogan grabbed Big John's leg, only to be kicked by the Studd's other leg. Hogan dropped to the floor.

Big John jumped out of the ring, picked up the Hulk, and tossed him into the ring like a sack of flour. Hogan, now flat on his stomach, seemed totally helpless. With the crowd urging the Hulk to get up, Big John Studd slowly climbed on the ropes and flew off them, slamming into the Hulk's back. He coaxed the dazed

Hulk to his feet before whipping him into the ropes. As Hogan rebounded, Studd crushed him with a fist to the head. Hogan collapsed. Studd, seizing his chance, went for the pin. But then as he heard the crowd shouting encouragement, Hulkamania began to inspire Hogan. Somehow, Hogan flipped Big John off at the count of two.

Big John Studd wanted this champion to go down. He picked up Hogan, threw him again onto the ropes, and met the stumbling Hulk with a clothesline blow to the throat. Somehow, the Hulkster again fought off another Studd pin attempt.

The End of the Hulk?
Now Big John and the worried crowd thought that the end of Hulk's reign was near. Studd picked up Hogan and easily slammed him into the canvas. Some people in the stands wept as they feared their hero was finished. As Studd strutted around the ring, Hogan slowly got to his feet only to have a Studd drop-kick hit him in the head. The kick was so effective that Hulk Hogan was sent right out of the ring.

The crowd came to life. The American Dream was in big trouble and needed a big dose of good ol' Hulkamania!

As Hogan tried to reenter the ring, Big John tried to kick him again. Hogan grabbed Studd's leg and pulled him out of the ring. Studd recovered quickly and pounded the champ on the back of the head.

The Slamming of Studd

Then it happened. Somehow Hogan reached down deep inside and found his secret formula – Hulkamania. He gritted his teeth and screamed at Studd, "Go on, hit me with your best shot!"

As Studd came in with the blow, Hogan blocked it and countered with a chop to Studd's forehead. Studd spun round from the force of the blow. Hogan jumped at the confused challenger, lifted him up, and – much to the approval of the delirious crowd – slammed Big John out of the ring and onto the concrete floor. Big John was so seriously injured that he was incapable of moving.

As the crowd roared, the Hulk waved his belt in victory. Not only had he defended his title, but he had also done what no wrestler had ever done before – Hulk Hogan had slammed Big John Studd! Hulkamania lives!

Bring on the Russian—
Hogan Beats Nikolai Volkoff

One problem that is created by the constant matching of good guys with bad guys is that sometimes a promoter runs out of one of the two categories. Early in 1985, still remaining one of the good guys, Sgt. Slaughter defected from the World Wrestling Federation due to the lack of a title shot. Also, two other heroes, Barry Windham and Mike Rotundo linked up to make a tag team, eventually winning the WWF belt.

The result was that promoters such as Vince McMahon, Jr., found that there weren't enough respected heroes to throw at the growing ranks of villains. As the predicament became more apparent, villains like the Iron Sheik, Big John Studd, and Nikolai Volkoff all lined up waiting for America's shining hope—who else but Hulk Hogan?

The patriotism that swept through the ranks of professional wrestling fans craved matches against the symbols of America's enemies. Despite the fact that Hogan doesn't go so far as to lead the crowd in the Pledge of Allegiance as Slaughter did, he still has been inspiring.

The Russian Menace

In April of 1985, Hulk battled the Russian Menace, Nikolai Volkoff. Volkoff stands six feet eight inches tall and weighs 345 pounds. There is no friendship lost between the two men. In the eyes of Mr. Hulkamania, there's no room for a person who ridicules the American way.

Similarly, Volkoff holds no love for the Hulkster. Big, blond, and brassy, Hogan represents the quintessential American male. The Russian threat, having been brought up under the cold, harsh Soviet regime, resents the image that Hulk Hogan represents — money and fame.

Since few American patriots are on the WWF scene to fight the notorious villains, it takes someone with Hogan's dedication to Hulkamania to defend our pride. Wrestling columnist Matt Brock sums up the situation. "I don't understand people's surprised reactions. Hulk Hogan's commitment to excellence is legendary. That he would pick up the cause of patriotism shouldn't surprise anyone. As champion, he understands the importance of maintaining the American system of life. As an American, his national pride is certainly wounded by the antics of foreign animals like Nikolai Volkoff."

But the more popular the Hulk becomes, the harder it is for him to meet the demands of wrestling promoters and his fans. In any given week the Hulk faces the likes of Roddy Piper, Big John Studd, the Iron Sheik, and Paul "Mr. Wonderful" Orndoff. Hogan had to come up with special added strength that week in 1985 because his opponent was Nikolai Volkoff.

Perhaps the Hulk was able to draw from his inner reserves after having to listen to Volkoff's less-than-stirring rendition of the Russian National Anthem.

The Match

The match started out as many professional bouts do. The action swung back and forth, with each man getting in a few good kicks to the other's head. As the match went on, it became apparent that the fatigue factor resulting from fighting four times that week was catching up with Hogan. Nikolai Volkoff began to hammer the Hulk with a vicious series of bear hugs and backbreakers. Volkoff was able to repeatedly pick up the champ and body slam him down to the mat.

Volkoff became so confident that he began taunting the battered Hulk as he tossed him around the ring. The crowd tried to give Hogan that extra lift with chants of "Hogan...Hogan!"

Then it happened as it had so many times before. Just when the situation seemed darkest

Nikolai Volkoff grips the Hulk in the dreaded backbreaker hold.

and Volkoff was close to winning — Hulkamania raised its beautiful head. Hogan took a deep breath and with one last-ditch effort hit Volkoff with a shattering forearm to the head. As the Russian staggered, Hogan somehow picked him up and slammed him to the canvas. Hogan finally put an end to the Russian with a flying elbow to the neck. Volkoff writhed in pain as Hogan applied the pressure needed for the pin.

Victorious again and with America's pride intact, Hulk Hogan waved his belt and went into his muscle-flexing victory dance.

The Hulk Meets Cowboy Bob Orton

Not only must Hulk Hogan defend his title against foreign challengers, but sometimes he also faces villains from his own backyard. The bad and the ugly need not speak with a foreign tongue. Take, for example, the notorious exploits of a bad guy, Cowboy Bob Orton.

By the sound of his name, one might assume that Cowboy Bob is another true-blue honest American. But don't be deceived. Orton's reputation is based on his violent, harmful tactics. Like a shark, Cowboy Bob seems to thrive on injured opponents.

The Squeeze

Even Hogan has become aware that the constant challenge by these villainous opponents might be taking its toll. As he told *Pro Wrestling Illustrated*, "As long as you're in control of the situation, everything is fine. But once the situation becomes bigger than you are, when you have to constantly run to be bigger and better than you were last time, you're doomed."

Has the phenomenon of Hulkamania gotten too big for Hogan to handle? How hard can he continually push himself? In Hogan's own words, "In nature, if you try to squeeze too much into a container it's bound to explode. The more you squeeze, the bigger the explosion. There is just so much energy a man can contain within a situation."

One wrestling commentator told *Wrestling USA*, "Right now, Hulkamania is running too wild, forcing Hogan to do too many things, and an explosion is inevitable. I think we're going to see one magnificent match, the wrestling equivalent to a nova, and then Hogan's WWF title reign will be finished. He'll be burned out and Hulkamania will be extinguished."

The Match

In the match with Cowboy Bob Orton, Hogan seemed to test the limits of Hulkamania. But, as always, he emerged triumphant. He almost

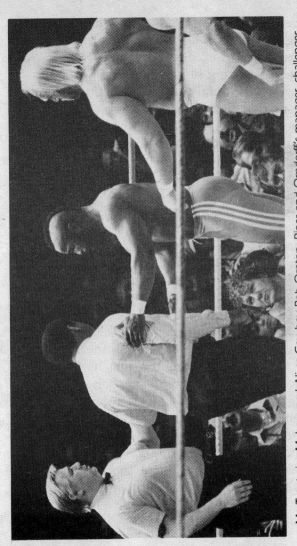

Mr. T restrains Muhammad Ali as Cowboy Bob Orndon, Piper and Orndoff's manager, challenges the former heavyweight boxing champion at the Madison Square Garden event, Wrestlemania.

dared Orton to use his most wicked tactics. Hogan took risks like turning his back on the advancing Orton. Several times Orton came close to inflicting serious harm on the Hulk.

Maybe the Hulk has a built-in timing mechanism that warns him when he has to get serious. In the Orton match, the clock went off after Hogan had been writhing in pain after a series of crushing body slams. Hogan's revenge came as he pummeled Orton with a series of forearms to the head. The Hulk then got his revenge by slamming Cowboy Bob onto the canvas near the edge of the ring. As the crowd roared approvingly, the Hulk bent Orton's dangerous left arm back along the ring apron.

As Orton writhed in pain, he asked the referee to stop the match. Victory again came for Hulkamania and its fans. The crowd leapt to their feet, clapping their hands to the now-familiar beat of the song "Eye of the Tiger."

Still in pain from the match, the Hulk waved his WWF championship belt around the ring. Once back in the locker room, the Hulk seemed to be feeling fine, avidly recalling his victory to the awaiting press. It was only after watching him limp away to his car that one sensed the possible threat that the rigorous trials of Hulkamania might pose for Hogan.

★ ★ ★ ★ ★ **CHAPTER FOUR** ★ ★ ★ ★ ★

The Good, the Bad, and the Ugly— Hulk's Rivals and Foes

Andre the Giant

In the world of professional wrestling it's getting hard to tell some of the good guys from the bad. It used to be that if you looked big and mean, the promoters automatically hyped you as a villain. Not so anymore. Intimidating physical specimens such as Hulk Hogan and Sgt. Slaughter have turned in their previous villain labels and taken up sides with the good guys.

That brings us to Andre the Giant. Today, at seven feet five inches and 497 pounds, not a soul alive would question his giant status. Andre is a true favorite of the fans. Since he wrestles in so many different areas of the country (he travels on the road about eleven months a year), he's never concentrated on simply maintaining a regional ranking. Without a regional ranking, there can be no championship.

On the Move

But not having a title belt doesn't bother the gentlemanly giant. As he relates in *The Pictorial History of Wrestling*, "My schedule demands that I am constantly on the move, and so I don't have time to keep up my regional ranking. I have had some championship bouts, but they either end at the time limit or the champ gets himself disqualified, because he'd rather lose the match than his belt."

In a feature article in *Sports Illustrated*, the Giant told what his travels have meant to his fans. "Sure, I'm on the road more often than not. But I really enjoy it. This sport has given me the opportunity to do whatever I want. I've made friends around the world and I've become quite an expert on restaurants. There are very few cities that haven't tried to keep me well fed."

The Giant and the Hulk

Since Andre the Giant is such a crowd favorite, how does he relate with another superhero—Hulk Hogan? Interestingly, the two wrestled as a tag team. The crowd went wild in Montreal as the Hulk and the Giant emerged victorious against the villains Blackjack Mulligan and Ken Patera. They were as indestructible as the Twin Towers in New York City. Although successful in the ring, the tag-team partnership soon disbanded.

The Hulk and Andre put on a post-match dressing room display that could have been entitled Clash of the Titans. Keep in mind that Andre had been involved with professional wrestling long before Hulk Hogan came on the scene. In fact, the early Hogan, under the guidance of Freddie Blassie, was billed as a villain. It was only three years ago that the then-evil Hogan had tried to break Andre's back in the ring.

Considering their early rivalry, it's hardly surprising that their existence as a tag team was shortlived. Before their tag-team match in Montreal, one noted wrestling promoter mused, "Hogan and Andre might be teamed now, but I can't believe these guys like or trust each other." He went on to relate in *Pro Wrestling Illustrated*, "They were enemies for years, the

Former tag-team partners Andre the Giant and Hulk Hogan plan strategy before a match.

bitterest kind. Even when they were supposedly friends, you could always feel the tension. They're an explosion waiting to happen."

In an article in *Wrestling Revue*, one commentator recalled the bout between Hogan and Andre three years earlier in Chicago. "Before they get touted as the world's greatest tag-team partners, I think everyone should consider the Chicago Battle Royal. These two went after each other like bitter enemies. It was an awe-inspiring sight. I swore the building shook. They may claim to be friends but they were looking to mix it up that night." It's not surprising that a Battle Royal, a no-holds-barred event where a group of wrestlers battle in the ring against each other, often produces heated confrontations.

In the dressing room after the Chicago bout, one promoter explained, "You could hear their voices shouting. They were calling each other some names that made me blush. They were totally out of control. I couldn't provide enough security if those two decided to turn on each other in a match."

The rivalry between the two has become legendary. Competing for the love of the crowd puts your ego on the line. The pride factor is the probable cause of the Hogan-Andre split-up.

Another promoter told *The Wrestler*, "You're dealing with very proud men here. Neither one is able to watch his partner grab all the glory. It wouldn't take much for one to think the other is putting him in the shadows. Neither man could tolerate that. That's where the explosion would start. I'm not sure they'd mean it, but it's bound to happen."

As fellow wrestler Sgt. Slaughter also told *The Wrestler* at the time, "I wouldn't want to be in the same room the first time Hulk and Andre lost. Neither man is used to it. Andre has never lost a match, and I think the blame would be flying fast and thick. I don't think it would be confined to a polite discussion over what went wrong. I wouldn't want to be around when that happens. I wouldn't suggest anybody be around."

And what does the main attraction of Hulkamania have to say about his partnership with Andre the Giant? In a *Pro Wrestling Illustrated* article he replied, "Everybody brings up the ego thing about every new team. Believe me, there's nothing to it. As for the Chicago thing, hey, I got hot, sure! I won't deny that. And I said some things I'm ashamed of. So did Andre. We both apologized later and forgot all about it." And as Hogan said, "A Battle Royal is a crazy place and crazy things happen. If you've been in the sport long enough, you know not to remember anything that happens during a Battle Royal."

The only party not heard from as yet is Andre the Giant. When asked about the reputed ego clash with the Hulk he replied, "I respect and admire Hulk Hogan. We could get better as we wrestle together. I don't go looking for trouble, and if I thought there was any danger of us not wrestling well together, I wouldn't do it. Hogan is the same way."

Asked about the Battle Royal in Chicago that prompted their animosity, Andre said, "Yeah, I remember the Battle Royal. We were both stupid. We won't be stupid again."

Andre may be the biggest professional wrestler in the business, but he also is the biggest gentleman.

Bob Backlund

In the world of professional wrestling where almost every grappler exploits a gimmick to attract the fans, there still exists a no-frills superstar.

No Frills
Unlike most professional wrestlers, Backlund started out as a college star. In the early 1970s he won the prestigious NCAA championship.

During his college career, he was named All-American four times. As he told reporter and wrestling expert Bert Randolph Sugar, "I've been wrestling for as long as I can remember."

After college, he was approached by the famous midwestern wrestling promoter Verne Gagne, who persuaded Backlund to turn pro. He wrestled all over the country. Then on February 20, 1978, in New York's Madison Square Garden, Backlund defeated Superstar Billy Graham and became the World Wrestling Federation Champion.

Backlund held the crown for nearly six years, defeating such challengers as Big John Studd, Sgt. Slaughter, and Greg Valentine. Then in a controversial bout, Backlund lost the crown to the Iron Sheik. The Sheik, of course, held the belt for only a short time, losing to the present WWF champion, Hulk Hogan.

The White Towel

Backlund's loss to the Iron Sheik was very controversial — someone literally tossed a white towel in the ring. The long-standing principle in the sport is that the title can only be won on a pin or a submission. This match had neither, yet Backlund was stripped of his title. Later he told this story to Bill Apter of *Pro Wrestling Illustrated*. "I felt that I didn't lose the championship. I felt that I lost the belt. They can take the belt away from me, but they can't take the title away. You have to be pinned or you have to submit, and that's been the rule in professional wrestling as long as I've been in it. Anybody that's ever lost the title since the WWF has started has lost by a pin or submission. If I got beat one-two-three, I'd have said, 'Okay, I'm gonna go home, train harder, I'm gonna try to figure out what mistake I made.' But that didn't happen. I still feel like I have the title. I just don't have the belt."

Backlund and the Hulk

After losing the belt, Backlund was matched with a tag-team partner who was quickly becoming a rising star. This rising star was Hulk Hogan. Backlund began to realize that the WWF was grooming Hogan for his eventual title shot against the Sheik. Backlund told Bill Apter, "I resented Hogan. There's a lot of people that have been in the WWF for a lot of years, and it seems like the guy that comes in and is in the WWF for two weeks [Hogan] doesn't deserve a shot as much as a guy who's proved himself for the last five years or even ten years."

One thing that can be said about Bob Backlund is that he's a wrestling technician. Go to any Backlund match and you see every maneuver in the book. Atomic knee drops, double-leg takedowns, and even aerial acrobatics.

Sgt. Slaughter wants you!

Pro Wrestling Illustrated asked Bob Backlund about his opinion of Hulk Hogan's skill as a wrestler. "He's a professional wrestler and I've gotta respect everybody in professional wrestling, because it takes a lot of hard work and determination, and the fans really like him. That's why he rose so quickly. Maybe they were tired of me, and the WWF had to find another hero to take the belt away from the Sheik."

Backlund, however, is not impressed with Hogan as a master of wrestling maneuvers. "I technically look at his matches and I guess the people could do the same thing, and you don't see him do too many wrestling maneuvers. That's what I look at to see if somebody is a great scientific wrestler. But I can't put him down, he's very successful in what he does."

Sgt. Slaughter

Just when the average American professional wrestling fan was yearning to express patriotic feelings, Sgt. Slaughter entered the ring. This ex-Marine comes complete with fatigues and a camouflaged car. At first, wrestling fans lived in fear of the Sarge and resented his abrupt, drill-instructor lessons. Then as he began to react to the pro-Iranian antics of the Iron Sheik, Americans flocked to his side in support. Even though it's Hulk Hogan who stripped the Sheik of the WWF title, Sgt. Slaughter is the one who directed his actions at "the open sore that flaunts in the face of Uncle Sam."

Waving the Flag

Whenever the Sheik and Slaughter take up a match the action gets very savage. Sgt. Slaughter gets quite mad everytime the Sheik approaches the ring waving the Iranian flag. As he told *The Pictorial History of Wrestling,* "I want that manager, the so-called Ayatollah Blassie and his Iranian maggot as well as all the other detractors from this great country beaten out of the ring — and out of the country. If this ends my career as a wrestler, I'll leave the ring a happy man."

Slaughter is such a patriot that as he approaches the ring he hands out American flags. His patriotism knows no bounds. He appeared in commercials plugging the United States Olympic Team. More recently, he has been seen on television commercials asking for donations to clean up the Statue of Liberty. He stands before the Statue, points and proclaims, "She's my favorite lady."

The Cobra Clutch

Every so often a wrestler develops a hold so lethal that its reputation lasts long after his retirement. Killer Kowalski had his Claw Hold. Sgt. Slaughter gets law and order with the famed Cobra Clutch. He has used the hold to beat powerful opponents like Nikolai Volkoff and the Sheik. To use the Cobra Clutch takes a special kind of God-given physical ability. It not only requires great phsyical strength but unusually long arms. Slaughter, in *Wrestling Super Stars*, said, "Of all the holds, the Cobra Clutch may be the most draining." The Cobra Clutch shows no mercy. But as the Sarge says, "The only people who suffer from the hold are the ones who deserve to suffer."

The Junkyard Dog

Professional wrestling fans begin clapping their hands before he ever leaves the dressing room. They rise to their feet upon hearing the first few bars of his now famous theme song, "Another One Bites the Dust." He, like Hulk Hogan, is one of wrestling's popular figures. He's known as JYD, but to the wrestling world he's the Junkyard Dog.

He has fought and beat every bad dude in the business. As he told Vince McMahon on *TNT*, "I'll take on everything. There is no dog in this Dog."

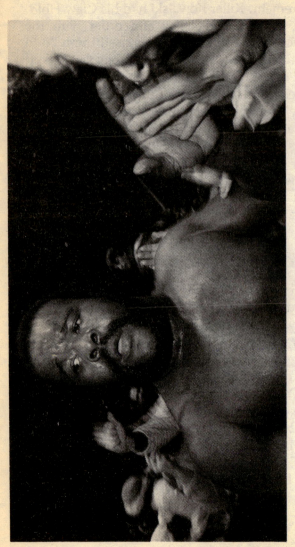

The Junkyard Dog approaches the ring, welcoming the chance to make another opponent "bite the dust."

During his career he has won the North American heavyweight championship and the Mid South tag-team title.

Favorite of the Fans

What makes him a favorite of the fans is the combination of his wrestling and his very engaging personality. As he approaches the ring for a match, he'll join the clapping fans as they sing his theme song. If there's a child nearby, he'll pick him up and put him in the ring. Then break dancing to the delight of the fans, the Junkyard Dog gives the child a taste of stardom by parading him around the ring.

Wrestling has been a shot in the arm to this ambassador of pleasure. He told *Wrestling* magazine, "The only thing that scares me is retirement. It's more than the wrestling itself that I'll miss, it's the life of a wrestler that means so much to me."

On *TNT* he once said, "Before I was a wrestler, my sense of self-respect was zero. I couldn't help myself or anybody that I loved. Then I suddenly became a mat star and suddenly the world was a wonderful place. I was cheered for doing what I do best. People got excitement from watching me. I was doing well, doing good!"

It's his genuine love of children that endears him to the fans. On his off days, he visits sick children in hospitals. "It's hard to describe the joy a man gets by visiting sick kids in the hospital. It never ceases to astonish me that meeting me can make a sick child feel better. That's a gift more precious than any wrestling title in the world."

His reciprocal love of his fans is very obvious whenever he wrestles. As one of professional wrestling's favorite heros, the Junkyard Dog welcomes the chance to join Hulk in an assault on the villains of the sport.

Roddy Piper

"Rowdy" Roddy Piper has become the most hated villain in professional wrestling. He's famous for the verbal abuse that he throws at his opponents. In fact, he even has a wrestling talk show entitled *Piper's Pit*. Wrestlers invited to be on the show as guests become victims of Piper's humiliating insults.

On *Piper's Pit*, Rowdy has a forum to brag from. "I'm a shrewd dude. I have tricks that nobody has ever seen. Some of these guys are so weak-minded that I've never had to really exert myself to kick them out of the ring. Some of the fans hate me, but you know what I think?

I know I'm good, and I don't need them to tell me so."

Kilts and Bagpipes

The thirty-three-year-old Piper has been wrestling as a professional since 1967. Born in Glasgow, Scotland, Piper attended high school in Manitoba, Canada. During his stay in Canada, Piper won the amateur wrestling championship. At sixteen, he was the youngest professional wrestler in Canada. Four years later, the twenty-year-old became the lightweight champion of the world, achieving that status at the youngest age ever. Perhaps that's where Rowdy's arrogance comes from.

It's hard to forget Rowdy's entrance into the ring. He wears a colorful kilt and at times plays his bagpipes.

During his professional wrestling career, he has wrestled almost every good guy in the book. He has many long-standing feuds with some of the sport's popular figures. Among others, Jimmy "Superfly" Snuka and Hulk Hogan are his arch rivals.

Since Rowdy Roddy is the host of his own talk show, perhaps we'll let the Piper play his own bag.

Rowdy Roddy Piper gets ready to smash an electric guitar in the ring. Piper proclaimed, "I hate rock 'n' roll!"

Piper's Pit

As an example of Rowdy's treatment of some of his wrestling colleagues on *Piper's Pit* one only has to point to the Jimmy "Superfly" Snuka segment. When Snuka was introduced, he emerged wearing his tropical native garb. The kilt-wearing Piper began taunting Snuka by offering him a banana and coconut. When the angered Snuka asked, "Are you making fun of me?" Piper replied by smashing the coconut over Snuka's head.

The coconut incident led to a bloody brawl in Madison Square Garden. At one point in the match, Piper threw Snuka headfirst out of the ring and then followed up by smashing a metal chair over his neck. Snuka was carried out of the ring on a stretcher.

On a recent segment of ABC's New York *Morning Show*, Rowdy spoke with Regis Philbin. "Me a villain?" Rowdy chuckled. "My mom doesn't think so. I have an image, you know, of always bragging, always boasting, but hey, pal, I'm the next superstar of wrestling, so they better get into it."

Lately, he has also become a manager for a few wrestlers, most notably Bad Bad Leroy Brown. Regarding his managerial talents, Rowdy Roddy told *Wrestler Annual*, "I know some punks think I'm too young to manage.

Rowdy Roddy Piper applies the deadly Sleeper Hold on Hulk Hogan. Hogan survived the maneuver to rise again and defeat Piper.

Why? If you have the brains, what difference does age make? You think I want my brain hardened like these other doddering fools? Man, I'm the greatest and I want to succeed in every sphere."

It's not hard to imagine why Piper has received so many threats. Recently he hired Cowboy Bob Orton, now known as "Ace," to be his bodyguard.

The Piper's Plan

Of course, Rowdy's ultimate plans must include taking the World Wrestling Federation title away from Hulk Hogan. Captain Lou Albano, an old pro when it comes to management and guile, believes he sees through Rowdy's smoke screen and out-of-the-ring actions. Albano, in *Wrestling's Main Event,* had this to say: "Roddy Piper has a plan, brother, and it did have merit, but due to his excitable personality, lack of managerial experience, and overall total incompetence he blew it!…The entire management thing and his *Piper's Pit* were just a smoke screen to help him get the belt. If he wants to accomplish this, he's got to stop playing around so much and head right towards the goal: Hulk Hogan!"

Nikolai Volkoff yells at the booing crowd.

Nikolai Volkoff

The bad guys just keep coming. This bearish Russian weighs 325 pounds. He has a sixty-five-inch chest, twenty-four-inch neck and twenty-three-inch arms. His is one bear hug smart wrestlers stay away from.

From the moment he enters the ring, the crowd boos. Soon against the crowd noise Volkoff proudly sings the Russian national anthem. "I sing out of respect for Motherland," grunts Volkoff to Jacqueline Quartarano of *Wrestling All Stars.* "Americans should pay attention, for soon all will be singing anthem as it will be anthem of whole world."

The Red Threat

Who brought this Red Threat to the wrestling world? Who else—Freddie Blassie. Blassie introduced Volkoff in 1974, and from the outset it was clear that Nikolai's strategy was aimed at showing those "soft Americans" who is boss.

Volkoff worked his way up to being the number one contender for Bruno Sammartino's WWF title. Wrestling fans will remember the series of battles between the two. One time he battled Sammartino to a fifty-four-minute draw ending at the 11:00 curfew.

Frustrated, Volkoff left the professional wrestling world. He returned in 1976 as a tag-

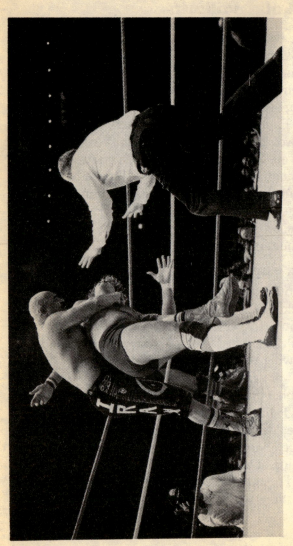

The Iron Sheik prepares to bring Barry Windham to his knees.

team partner of Japan's Tor Kamata, and together they destroyed opponents. Just as the team was reaching its peak, Volkoff returned again to Russia.

For some reason, he came back to the United States; and this time, with his tag-team partner Chris Markoff, Volkoff won the Mid-Atlantic and Florida titles.

Now rippling with success, Volkoff wreaked havoc in Japan, Australia, and Hong Kong. Just as the American fans thought they'd seen the last of Volkoff, he reappeared in July 1983 and has stayed ever since. Why did he so often leave the United States? Nikolai Volkoff answered in *The Pictorial History of Wrestling,* "I had grown weak and weary of being around nothing but American losers. I'm back to rule the world like my Russian ancestors."

Still under Blassie's thumb, Volkoff is paired with the Iron Sheik as one of the most formidable tag teams to challenge Hulk Hogan.

The Iron Sheik

Not only is the Iron Sheik bad, but he also is not the best-looking guy in the world. But what he lacks in looks he makes up for in wrestling expertise. In 1972, he won a gold medal representing Iran in the Munich Olympic Games. In the following years, he also competed in the Pan American Games, the Asian Games, and the European Games.

Since becoming a professional he has held many titles including the European heavyweight, the Canadian belt, and the World Wrestling Federation title – until he was beaten by Hulk Hogan.

The Iron Sheik's first entrance to the WWF was made in 1974, by his new manager – Freddie Blassie. Blassie was so caught up with the success of his Iranian champ that he began referring to himself as "The Ayatollah."

Blassie hooked up with the Sheik because "I knew that with his wrestling background, his hunger, his desire, he would be a world champion. I once asked the Sheik what his mission in life was and he said, 'I want to cripple, humble, and humiliate all the weak Americans and to prove, once and for all, my worth as champion.'"

The Camel Clutch

The Sheik developed the dreaded Camel Clutch, a hold that no wrestler, except of course Hulk Hogan, has ever escaped from. When he sits on an opponent's back, reaches under their arms, and pulls on the chin with his massive hands, the result is almost always submission.

Blassie's Baddles

When asked to compare the tag-team partners, Blassie told *Wrestling All Stars*, "The Iron Sheik has won championships all over the world. He did what no man could do for five years, he beat the all-American wimp, Bob Backlund. Volkoff has wrestled all over, even behind the Iron Curtain.

"Not only do my men have the skill, stamina and strength, they have experience and they have a secret weapon no other team in the world has, me! They've got the brains of Freddie Blassie working for them!"

The Sheik knows how valuable Blassie is for his career. "Ayatollah Blassie is very wise man. He has told Mr. Nikolai Volkoff and Iron Sheik that we will be tag-team champions and we are. That we will destroy Sgt. Slaughter, Hulk Hogan, that punk Sammartino's kid, and everyone! We will wrestle until we simply own all the championships. Then we will return to our motherlands with all these titles."

"Ayatollah Blassie" doesn't feel like he's sold out America as he directs the Sheik's attack. "Me a traitor? That shows how ignorant you pencil-necked geeks are. I love America, especially good old American cash. With the greatest tag team in history, Nikolai Volkoff and the Iron Sheik, I'll be the richest American you ever saw."

As Cyndi Lauper would say...Money changes everything!

CHAPTER FIVE

Boys Just Wanna Have Fun— Rock'n'Roll Wrestling

The whole entertainment world has gone mad. Turn on rock 'n' roll stations like MTV and you see live professional wrestling matches from Madison Square Garden. But you wanted to hear some music, so you channel hop to a network's Friday night videos. Looking closely you realize that the voices booming from the videos belong to wrestling managers Captain Lou Albano and Freddie Blassie instead of Mick Jagger and Huey Lewis.

Trying to regain your composure, you decide that if they're going to bombard the airwaves with grapplers you might as well watch a wrestling show. So with your trusty remote in hand, you whip over to one of the many nationally ranked cable wrestling shows. Tears of frustration well up in your eyes, as rockers Cyndi Lauper and George Thorogood gab about their love of professional wrestling. What happened?

The New Tag Team

What happened is the biggest merger in entertainment history since rock met roll! Rock 'n' roll has joined with professional wrestling to become the greatest tag-team partnership of all time. Daily this tandem is putting a stranglehold on the multimillion-dollar entertainment business. As that old rocker Al Einstein might have said, "It's a classic example of the sum being greater than the parts!"

Cyndi Lauper properly evaluated the effect wrestling has had. She told NBC's *SportsWorld*, "Wrestling is breaking wide open. It's no longer just an underground thing. It's helped me on my outlook on things. It's taught me a lot about what I need to do to keep myself in shape for rock 'n' roll!"

Wrestlers are coming out of the woodwork trying to associate themselves with rock songs. Hulk Hogan enters the ring to "Eye of the Tiger." The Junkyard Dog drives the crowds wild as he break dances to "Another One Bites the Dust." The tag-team match of Barry Windham and Mike Rotundo have adopted Bruce Springsteen's "Born in the USA" as their song. Wrestlemania has met Musicmania!

Cyndi Lauper and Lou Albano

Where did it all start? Without a doubt it began with the respective industries' odd couple – 100-pound rocker Cyndi Lauper and 300-pound wrestling manager Captain Lou Albano.

Cyndi was a struggling young rock singer full of fantasies of fame and, in her own words, "willing to do anything to make it" when – like many great couples – they met by accident. In *The Cyndi Lauper Scrapbook*, she recalls that first meeting. "I met Lou on a plane coming back from Puerto Rico. I recognized him right away because my Grampa Gallo loves wrestling. We started talking and he decided that I could be a champion, and since he's a maker of champions, he got involved in my career as my personal and technical advisor. It's important for every rock 'n' roller to have one of these role models. And he is *some* role model to have."

Cyndi Lauper followed up on her new-found friendship with Albano, one of wrestling's biggest notables. She began roaming around wrestling events at Madison Square Garden whenever matches were held. With her distinctive looks security guards began viewing her as a safe regular, and soon Ms. Lauper wound up backstage talking to her new idols, Albano and wrestlers like Hulk Hogan.

The PEG Principle

After a series of meetings with Captain Lou, she was able to convince him that she needed his management to get her career off the ground. During the following weeks, Albano taught Cyndi what he called the PEG Principle. The acronym stands for Politeness, Etiquette, and Grooming. It seems hard to believe that Albano, a man who wears rubber bands in his cheek, could be a disciple of PEG, but in any event it seemed to work for his tag-team wrestlers.

Cyndi told authors Marie Morrente and Susan Mitteklauf what PEG means to her career: "People are reading about it everywhere and they're asking me, what's this Politeness, Etiquette, and Grooming thing. These are things very important to musicians. We all have to try very hard to be polite. It doesn't come easy given what we go through. And since we have to do a lot of business over lunches, you know, maybe with people like record company presidents, we have to have etiquette, we have to know which fork to pick up. And nobody has better grooming than Lou. Nobody knows how to eat better than he does. He manages the Samoans, and they're well coiffed, which is a key part of grooming. And their costumes are wonderful. Their togas come from Paris."

She's So Unusual

Perhaps because of Captain Lou's advice or maybe simply because her time had finally arrived, Cyndi cut her first hit album, *She's So Unusual*. The record company decided to release two videos for the album: "Time After Time" and the now-famous "Girls Just Wanna Have Fun." The Captain gave Cyndi some advice on the videos. Soon he was cast in what has become one of rock video's most recognizable supporting roles. Captain Lou plays Cyndi's admonishing, unkempt father in "Girls."

Lou Albano had spent over thirty years in the wrestling business. Many baby-boomers, now heavily into rock 'n' roll, recognized the Captain in Cyndi's video. All over the country

Cyndi Lauper looks worried as she watches Lelani Kai battle Wendi Richter.

people laughed with recognition as they pointed out Albano's cameo role. Aided by Albano's appearance and Cyndi's animated style of song and dance, the "Girls" video caused her record sales to skyrocket. The video was shown almost hourly on MTV. For a few months it seemed that every radio station in America had fallen in love with the *She's So Unusual* album. The Lou and Lauper connection was etched in platinum!

The Feud

What followed this success was a year-long feud that at times rivaled the Jerry Lewis–Dean Martin debacle of the 1960s. Cyndi took on a new manager, Dave Wolff. Albano began using the wrestling talks shows to take shots at his "creation," Cyndi Lauper. They both used the press and news media to escalate the blowup into front-page news.

Captain Lou always had a reputation as a chauvinist. In anger, his old philosophy that "women belong at home getting pregnant" spilled out to the press, who gobbled up the gossip. Lou proclaimed, "I made her a music superstar. She was nothing without me."

Life magazine had run a spread on Lauper and Albano before the rift. The article showed how each had benefited form the other's area of expertise. Albano, on network news, pointed to the *Life* article and said, "See *Life* magazine? Without me, she'd be nothing. People reacted to me, Captain Lou, not her."

A calm Cyndi appeared in an interview saying, "I love Lou, but he's not my manager."

"Her brain's a dehydrated BB," Lou countered.

"He's got a calcium deposit and going crazy," Cyndi angrily stated when interviews asked about her "former" friend.

The feud made headlines, not only in the music and wrestling worlds, but also in the news media in general. On a daily basis, articles about wrestling and rock 'n' roll appeared in all the media. While Cyndi's album soared up the charts, Madison Square Garden began selling out to capacity crowds. The Hulk started using "Eye of the Tiger" as his theme song and female wrestler Wendi Richter came out of the dressing room as the loudspeakers played Lauper's "Girls Just Wanna Have Fun."

Whether the feud had been planned or not, it created a huge following. Dave Wolff told NBC's *SportsWorld*, "Rock 'n' Roll is extremely entertaining and energetic. When you put them together, you get something stronger than one or the other. It's a hybrid form that's turning on the masses."

As the feud heated up, professional wrestling promoter Vince McMahon, Jr., was too busy counting his gate receipts to watch MTV. Record companies eagerly encouraged other wrestlers to use rock songs as themes. George Thorogood, a popular rock leader, asked the Hulk to introduce him at a number of concerts.

The feud was being hyped on Roddy Piper's talk show, *Piper's Pit*. On one segment Cyndi appeared and challenged Lou to a wrestling match. No, it wasn't to be the 100-pound Cyndi against Albano. Instead Lauper offered to manage Wendi Richter in a match against Albano's client, the Fabulous Moolah.

The Richter-Moolah Match

The bout took place on July 23, 1984, at, of course, Madison Square Garden, and MTV covered the event live. Before the match, Lauper dismissed Captain Lou as a hanger-on, a man just trying to remain in the spotlight. Lou appeared on MTV claiming to have ghost-written "Girls" and "Time After Time."

The night of the match saw a crowd filled with wrestling enthusiasts. They were there to see the bouts, but more importantly, many wanted to show the music world what wrestling was all about. This was an informed, enthusiastic wrestling crowd that was chomping at the bit waiting to see rock 'n' roll's reaction to live wrestling.

Cyndi arrived in her usual PEG best... lime-green socks, green corset, and fishnets. Nothing like being well groomed!

This was a regular wrestling card, so the rockers were able to witness a few preliminary events. One of these pitted Greg Valentine against the champion, Hulk Hogan. After Hogan had dispatched Valentine, he stuck around to witness the upcoming media event.

As the crowd settled into their seats, Captain Lou and the Fabulous Moolah entered the ring. Moolah had been champion for twenty-six years and appeared determined to defeat the challenger, who was sponsored by "that nut Lauper."

As Lou timidly looked on, Moolah strutted around the ring radiating confidence. She wanted to show the world the finest in women's wrestling. Little did she realize she was about to get the shock of her life!

Finally Lauper and Richter made their way into the ring, greeted by thousands of wrestling fans. Wendi smiled brilliantly, excited by the opportunity to dethrone the Fabulous Moolah before this frenzied crowd and the live television hookup.

Rock star Cyndi Lauper excites the crowd as she joins wrestler Wendi Richter at ringside. Richter later defeated the Fabulous Moolah for the women's championship.

After all the weeks of hype and interviews, the match finally began. As soon as Richter and Moolah began mixing it up, they both realized that this night was going to be a real test of endurance. Moolah was in her most wicked mood. She raced across the ring and dragged Wendi by the hair. She continually used a series of painful blows, always aware of the position of the referee in the ring. Wrestling fans, although booing wildly at her tactics, had to be impressed by the way she hid them from the referee.

Leg locks and neck holds prevailed in the early stages of the match. Richter took the offensive in the middle of the match. She connected on a perfect drop-kick to Moolah's chest, driving her to the canvas. Wendi Richter seemed to be gathering strength as her confidence increased.

Meanwhile, Captain Lou looked stunned as he began to see the handwriting on the wall. He sensed that all this crazy publicity and the feud with Cyndi might cause Moolah to lose her title – a title she had held for almost three decades.

Cyndi was wildly cheering on Richter. As the match went on she exhorted the fans to get behind Wendi's efforts. At one point, she pointed to Albano and announced, "You're going down!"

The fans responded with a roar that even surprised the MTV personnel. The crowd began shouting for Wendi, hoping to see an end put to Moolah's stranglehold on the women's World Wrestling Federation title.

Toward the end of the match, Cyndi was no longer able to control herself. She jumped on the apron of the ring, brandishing what looked like a rolled up sock in her fist. Richter pulled the struggling Moolah over to Lauper. Cyndi grabbed Moolah. With a raised fist, Lauper looked around at the cheering fans waiting for their approval. They roared with support as Cyndi belted the surprised Fabulous One. She later said, "I didn't want to do it. But she got what she deserves. I mean, she's representing a man who abuses women. What does that make her? After I hit her, I felt a lot better!"

Moolah retaliated and took it out on Richter. After softening her up with a few blows to the head, it was time for the finale.

Moolah caught Wendi in a reverse cradle as they both tumbled to the canvas. Both of their backs were pinned to the mat. Like a boxing official counting out both fighters, the referee, Jack Lotz, began his count of three. Cyndi screamed for Richter to move off the mat. At the count of two, Wendi somehow managed to raise one shoulder. Moolah, who thought she had

Rock star Cyndi Lauper celebrates with the new WWF women's champion, Wendi Richter.

bridged her own shoulder off the mat, believed that the referee was counting out Richter.

At the count of three, Moolah jumped up, arms upraised, celebrating her "victory." She was absolutely stunned when the ring announcer told the crowd there was a *new* women's champion. Cyndi jumped into the ring, and the girls danced around as "Girls Just Wanna Have Fun" boomed out of the loudspeaker.

After the bout Wendi Richter told *Wrestling's Main Event*, "It's such a change to have everyone on my side. It just gave me so much energy. I now realized how many years I wasted thinking that breaking the rules would help me win. But now, Cyndi gave me inspiration. I trained. I sweated. I owe her a lot."

Cyndi replied, "Any woman can get what she wants. If she wants it bad enough, all she has to do is try hard!"

After twenty-six years, the reign of the Fabulous Moolah was over. She and Captain Lou screamed at the referee, but to no avail.

In the dressing room, the champagne flowed as Wendi celebrated with her friends, Sgt. Slaughter, Hulk Hogan, and Cyndi Lauper. Later at New York's vogue Chiaki Restaurant, MTV hosted a sushi party. The invitees were a Who's Who in the wrestling and rock worlds. Throughout the night Cyndi and Hulk Hogan mugged it up before the photographers.

In many ways the bout between Fabulous Moolah and Wendi Richter seemed to legitimize wrestling for the world. The World Wrestling Federation embraced Cyndi Lauper as a valuable asset.

Reconciliation

It was time to bury the hatchet. For the good of the sport, Captain Lou publicly apologized to Cyndi. The first apology came as a surprise. Lou stepped onstage at Pier 84 in New York City, grabbed the microphone, and apologized to Lauper prior to one of her rock 'n' roll performances.

On stage with Cyndi was her mother. In the audience were some of her fans from the wrestling world, including Hulk Hogan. In *Wrestling USA*, Albano was quoted as saying: "Now I'm not gonna go out there and make a fool of myself. I'm not gonna get down on my knees. I'm gonna say: Cyndi Lauper, I'm sorry for saying that all women were wimps, belonged in the household, were good for raising babies and cleaning the kitchen. All right, let's face it. I'm sorry. Women are good for many other things, they're on a level of a man. So I was wrong."

At this point, Cyndi walked across the stage

and the "odd couple" embraced. They then announced to the world that they were teaming up to raise money to fight multiple sclerosis. Captain Lou said, "Now that we're burying the hatchet, I'm getting together with Cyndi to raise money. As you know I was chosen as a judge in the Ugly Bartender contest. It's gonna be my pickings against Cyndi Lauper's. I feel that I'm qualified to talk about ugliness, and ugliness is involved with mulitple sclerosis...When I get up in the morning and look into a mirror, it takes me twenty minutes before I can brush my teeth, looking at an old ugly face like this. I've got over 700 stitches in my face, my nose has been fractured seven times. I wrote the book on ugly."

The Ugly Bartender Contest

Albano then said, "So I have decided to dedicate my time to the multiple sclerosis drive, and because of this I have made this public apology to Cyndi Lauper."

According to a press release issued from the New York City chapter of the National Multiple Sclerosis Society, the Ugly Bartender Contest is one of the MS Society's biggest fund-raising events. Patrons of local restaurants, lounges, pubs, and bars vote for their favorite "ugly" bartender by contributing money on-premises, each twenty-five-cent donation being worth one vote. UGLY has a positive connotation for bartenders: It stands for Understanding, Generosity, Lovable, and Youthful.

Roddy's Revenge

The match between Moolah and Richter, and the hype of Captain Lou's public apology, had a strange effect on the wrestling world. Albano has realigned himself in the wrestling world. Following the leads of Sgt. Slaughter and Hulk Hogan, Captain Lou has left the ranks of the notorious and aligned himself with the good guys, the fans' favorites. In so doing he has angered such old friends as Greg Valentine and Roddy Piper.

The whole event exploded in December of 1984. At Madison Square Garden, the World Wrestling Federation had planned a special night to honor Cyndi Lauper's "Contributions to Rock and Wrestling." At ringside were such notables as Wendi Richter, Dick Clark, Lou Albano, and Hulk Hogan.

Cyndi also had a gift for the World Wrestling Federation. She was going to present them with one of her platinum albums. The event was widely covered by the press. In the begin-

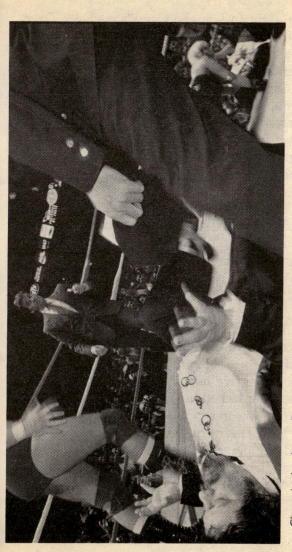

Chaos in the ring as Roddy Piper stalks a retreating Dick Clark. Earlier Piper attacked Lou Albano and Cyndi Lauper's manager, David Wolff.

ning, Captain Lou and Cyndi's manager, Dave Wolff, met in the center of the ring, shook hands, and thereby signaled the end of their bitter dispute over who is Cyndi's real manager.

Captain Lou then kissed Cyndi. Cyndi was holding one of her platinum records to give Albano. Then, from out of nowhere, who shows up but Rowdy Roddy Piper! As Dick Clark hastily backed away, Roddy grabbed Cyndi's framed platinum record and said, "Lou, you really deserve this and I want to be the one to give it to you!" Having said that, Roddy smashed the framed record over the unsuspecting Albano's head. As Albano dropped to the mat, Piper proclaimed that he, not Lou, was responsible for Lauper's success because of the exposure he gave her on *Piper's Pit*.

The guests began to flee the arena as Piper picked up Dave Wolff and body slammed him to the canvas. Cyndi rushed over to Wolff, trying to revive him. As she was leaning over him, Piper kicked her in the face. The scene in the ring was mayhem and very ugly.

Hulk Hogan rushed into the ring, grabbed hold of Piper, and threw him to the mat. From the audience, the television celebrity Mr. T also appeared, running to the ringside to cheer for Hogan. Piper and Hogan were slugging it out as

Hulk Hogan meets face-to-face with Mr. T of *The A Team*. Hogan later teamed up with Mr. T to battle Roddy Piper and Paul Orndorff for *Wrestlemania*'s main event.

a hundred policemen stormed the ring to re-store law and order.

Hogan and Piper continued to shout at each other. Mr. T slammed his fist into the ring with frustration. After Piper was removed from the arena, Hulk Hogan and Mr. T came to Cyndi's aid. Dave Wolff, now comatose, was put on a stretcher and carried out of the arena. With the celebrity-packed crowd in shock, Hogan and Mr. T vowed revenge on Rowdy Roddy and his evil friends.

They would get the opportunity to seek their revenge and defend Cyndi's honor on March 31, 1985, at Madison Square Garden in an event that was properly called Wrestlemania!

★ ★ ★ ★ ★ ★ **CHAPTER SIX** ★ ★ ★ ★ ★ ★

Welcome to Wrestlemania!

Satisfaction Guaranteed

The recipe is fairly simple. Start off with Hulk Hogan and his special, frenzied brand of entertainment called Hulkamania. Then add a grudge match featuring Cyndi Lauper and the Fabulous Moolah. Stir in a $15,000 body slam contest between arch enemies Andre the Giant and Big John Studd. Add a pinch of international flavor with Nikolai Volkoff and the Iron

Ring announcer Billy Martin and guest referee Muhammad Ali respond to the cheers of the Garden crowd.

A joyous Liberace watches the Hulk's posing routine as the
crowd roars with approval.

Sheik. For spice add Mr. T, Muhammad Ali, and Battling Billy Martin. Sweeten the pot with Liberace. Put the mixture in Madison Square Garden before a sold-out crowd. Then beat, stir, blend, punch, kick, and puree for three hours and voila...WRESTLEMANIA!

Wrestlemania took the world by storm on March 31, 1985. After one week of the heaviest publicity ever to hit the entertainment industry, 24,000 screaming, anxious professional wrestling fans descended upon the Garden to witness history. It was such an elaborate extravaganza that the World Wrestling Federation was rightly justified in using the phrase Wrestlemania. For this event was far more than your typical wrestling lineup. Seven preliminary bouts matched opponents right out of Who's Who in the wrestling world. These exciting preliminaries whipped the crowd into a frenzy, readying them for the grand finale — a tag-team match featuring the villains Rowdy Roddy Piper and Paul "Mr. Wonderful" Orndorff against America's hero Hulk Hogan and a new entry into the wrestling kingdom — Mr. T! Who could ask for anything more?

Outside the Garden, ticket scalpers were selling ringside seats for $300 each. Thousands of disappointed fans, unable to land a ticket, trudged home in the rain. Inside the arena people were busy snatching up Hulkamania and Wrestlemania T-shirts. Few could sit still in their seats.

Across the nation, one million viewers prepared to watch Wrestlemania on closed-circuit television. What had started out as a match to avenge the honor of Cyndi Lauper had become "The Brawl to Settle It All."

It's Show Biz

The publicity that preceded Wrestlemania had been awesome. Throughout the week, newspapers and television news programs presented little sketches of the participants. Thanks to the media blitz, even the first-time wrestling fan soon knew about Roddy Piper disgracing Cyndi by smashing one of her platinum records over the head of her friend, Captain Lou Albano. The tandem of Mr. T and Hulk Hogan appeared on such programs as *Entertainment Tonight* and NBC's *SportsWorld*. Mr. T was a guest on the *Late Night with David Letterman* show, where at one point, he snarled and said, "I'm a silly fool for even bein' here. I'm in training. This is serious. You can get hurt real bad in there if you're unprepared." As a topper to the publicity-filled week, Hulk Hogan and Mr. T guest hosted *Saturday Night Live*.

Mr. T and Hulk Hogan field questions as they promote Wrestlemania.

Earlier that week, Mr. T and Hulk Hogan conducted a series of late-night interviews that were hardly of the Meet the People format. Mr. T was never seen without a pair of work gloves, claiming "they keep my hands tough. For this type of dirty work you gotta be prepared for a street fight." Mr. T was on a special diet, eating only granola, wheat germ, and an oily honey mix. There was no need to offer him a plate; T, as the Hulk calls him, just spooned it right out of the jar. Mr. T stopped swallowing long enough to tell Sherryl Connelly of *The New York Daily News*, "I like rasslin' because it is so rough. I have always been involved in rasslin'. I like brutal sports. You gotta understand that even before I went to Hollywood I was the toughest bouncer. I was a top bodyguard, and I was a wrestlin' champion in Chicago."

Mr. T smashes his fists together, grabs his ever-trusty arm-strength developer, the "bull-whipper," and, flexing his impressive biceps, adds, "So I am no tennis player goin' into rasslin', you know."

On a *Live at Five* segment, Mr. T was asked what he felt about the new wrestling fans who are attracted by the merger of the sport with rock 'n' roll. He replied, "All these Yuppies, Yippies are a bunch of jerks. What did they ever do for fun? Sit in front of a computer and punch buttons? They used to put on disguises and sneak into rasslin' matches. Now they shell out the big bucks and sit ringside. The real rasslin' fan sweats for his pay. He's been comin' to watch these guys for years. Now he can't get in because the jackets and ties bought out the place."

On the *Late Night with David Letterman* show, Mr. T explained the sacrifice he made to get ready to team up with the Hulkster. Slapping his muscular abdomen he said, "I've completely cut out the unnecessaries. I'm missin' my donuts, my ice cream. My weight's down, I'm ready to rumble."

On television's popular show *The A Team* Mr. T is the big, bruising enforcer. But put him in the ring with people built like Hulk Hogan or Andre the Giant and, believe it or not, T becomes just part of the scenery. That's not to say he can't take care of himself.

Tag Team Theatrics

His coalition with the Hulk has created a new definition of workout. They have become the best of friends. Mr. T and Hulk Hogan first met on the set of Sylvester Stallone's *Rocky III*. In that movie, they played Clubber Lang and Thunderlips, respectively. Respectfully! Now as they physically prepare to batter the Piper-Orndorff combo, they have only compliments for each other. Mr. T told *The Daily News,* "Hulk taught me how to build up my muscles. I taught him how to get dirty. . . .We complement each other."

When Mr. T and Hulk Hogan get together for an interview, even Mike Wallace would have a hard time controlling the tempo. On *Entertainment Tonight,* the duo explained what preparations they were going through and how close they've become. The first part of the interview was conducted outdoors in Hogan's hometown of Venice, California. Venice is known as a major bodybuilding center. That became obvious as Mr. T began doing pull-ups with Hogan hanging from his back. "It was destiny that brought us together," said Mr. T. "We are the dream team. The best thing ever to happen to wrestling. And what we're gonna do on March 31 will be a shame."

Hogan leaned closer to the camera and in his familiar rapid-fire method of speaking said, "I don't see any way Piper and Orndorff are going to stop us. Ain't no way in the world. Not with all New York City, all the Hulkamaniacs behind us. Even with *Entertainment Tonight* behind us. . .how they're gonna stop the two stark raving maniacs?" Then looking at Mr. T, Hulk

After ripping off their Hulkamania T-shirts, Hogan and Mr. T prepare to batter their rivals. Orndorff and Piper at Wrestlemania.

said, "How 'bout that?"

As Hogan took in some air, Mr. T countered, "No way we get beat."

Saturday Night Shennanigans

Asked about why they were breaking their serious training to host NBC's *Saturday Night Live*, Mr. T offered, "We have to relax a little bit." Then, having just warmed up, Mr. T, with the Hulk laughing in the background, launched a verbal attack at the people in the entertainment business. "...there's a bunch of phony people out there in Hollywood. They're just like the cards they carry. They're plastic, not real. Everybody thinks they're a star. The only stars are up in heaven."

Comparing the Hollywood types to wrestlers, Mr. T added, "That's why I like wrestling."

Speaking about friendship and fair play, Hogan told *Entertainment Tonight*, "I've learned a lot from Mr. T. I've learned about loving, living, and survival....But the thing that Mr. T has taught me, when you get in a bind, man, when it gets rough and tough, you got to know how to throw that cheap shot, man. It's a matter of survival."

The Hulkamania crew of Muhammad Ali, Liberace, and Hulk Hogan pose during a prefight news conference.

Hulk Hogan, Superstar

All of the hype and publicity surrounding Wrestlemania has elevated Hogan to the status of superstar. The Hulkster, in an unusually subdued tone, told *The New York Daily News*, "It's hard for me to explain what it is like to be the Hulk. To be world champion, to be the number one wrestler and more importantly the number one draw. You can't just be a big, dumb wrestler. You're got to be able to walk and talk. You have to have something visual so that when people see you, they freak out. Plus you have to be smart."

Hulk Hogan appreciates the wedding of rock 'n' roll and wrestling. In fact, as we know, it was Hogan who stepped into the ring to prevent Roddy Piper from continuing his carnage on rock's diminutive superstar, Cyndi Lauper. Hogan understands the theatrics behind the music and the grappling. As he releated to Sherryl Connelly, "I am the best at both things. At wrestling. And theatricality. When I go out there and shake my hair and pose and flex my muscles, you hear people scream and yell; 20,000 people yell when I flex my arm!"

Walking on Broadway in New York City with ABC reporter John Stossel, Hulk said, "Hey, man, it's all for real." Flexing his massive arms, Hulk said to a woman who approached him. "Here touch it and hang on for your life!"

He has become the proverbial living legend. But some still dare to call him a fluke, an oddity, even a monster. To that the Hulk replied in *The New York Daily News*, "I take monster as a compliment, it doesn't mean something ugly to me. It means I can't be stopped. It means even other wrestlers can't believe how big I am. I'm thirty years old, rich and famous. If that's an oddity, I want more."

So much for the prefight publicity. The crowd is all warmed up. The Garden is packed. Let's take our seats and take in some Wrestlemania—Hulk Hogan style!

Greg "The Hammer" Valentine vs. The Junkyard Dog

The first thing that you notice about professional wrestling matches is that the bad dude, the villain, the guy you love to hate always enters the ring first. This gives the fans time to practice booing and allows the villain a chance to defile the audience.

Greg "The Hammer" Valentine, one of the wrestling game's dirtiest players, entered the ring wearing a sky blue robe. He immediately tossed the robe off and flexed around the ring. He sneered. He snarled. He fixed his golden hair.

Then a hush came over the crowd as if the whole scene had been rehearsed. And then it began. Spotlights lit up the ramp leading from the dressing room area to the ring. The crowd cheered as the Garden's intricate sound system began playing the familiar theme song of one of wrestling's most loved grapplers—the Junkyard Dog, also known as JYD. JYD bounced up the ramp, accompanied by the song "Another One Bites the Dust."

Unlike the standard robe worn by most wrestlers, JYD was wearing another of his trademarks: a heavy link metal chain wrapped around his shoulders and dangling down his back. With wild eyes he jumped up on the ring apron.

The crowd shouted as one, singing "Another One. . ." They were waiting for JYD's famous break dancing routine. Not one to disappoint an audience, he grabbed ropes around the ring, bent down at the knees, and with his head thrown back shimmied and shaked. It was just what the house wanted. . .at least for openers.

What the fans really wanted was for JYD to give a good old-fashioned thumping to the arrogant Valentine. It didn't take long.

Valentine took the lead early in the bout, throwing a few forearms at the Junkyard Dog.

The Junkyard Dog, wearing his traditional chains, break dances to "Another One Bites the Dust."

Valentine continued the assault by throwing JYD against the ropes and then clotheslining him on the rebound.

The tide turned as Valentine climbed up on the ropes and attempted a flying leap on the prone JYD. Just as Valentine was about to land his 250-pound flying frame on JYD's body, the Junkyard Dog rolled away. With a resounding thud, Valentine landed face-first on the mat.

Doing the Dog

Apparently stunned, Valentine was still able to get on all fours facing JYD. He looked up, and there was the Junkyard, also on his hands and knees, grinning at him. Before Valentine could react, JYD struck. Still on his hands and knees, he drove forward, smashing his forehead against Valentine's skull.

A dazed Valentine rolled away. Smiling, JYD rolled in the same direction, set himself, drove forward, and with a crashing thump he butted Valentine again.

The wrestling fans at the Garden were screaming with delight. For the older fans, it brought back memories of Bob Brazil's famous Cocoa Butt.

Four times Valentine rolled away, only to be follwed and then butted again by the grinning JYD.

Frustrated and probably suffering from the biggest headache in North America, Valentine crawled out of the ring, waving back in disgust at JYD.

As the referee counted Valentine out, JYD with arms raised, break danced around the ring to "Another One Bites The Dust." The world had a new InterContinental Heavyweight Champ!

Andre the Giant vs. Big John Studd

This was no ordinary wrestling match. For years Big John Studd had claimed that no man alive could slam him to the canvas. Many had tried, nobody had succeeded.

This time, Big John offered a special prize. Billed as "The $15,000 Slam Match," Studd offered the money in cash if Andre was successful. In return, it was announced at ringside that Andre would retire from wrestling if unsuccessful.

Prior to the event, Big John Studd was interviewed by Regis Philbin. He told ABC's New York *Morning Show* host, "Nobody has ever slammed me, so I had to offer money up front." Holding up a small duffle bag, Studd waved it at Philbin, who reached in and removed a few bills. Pulling the bag away, Studd laughed and said, "Hey let's not let it all fall out now! There's a lot of hungry people out there."

Seriously staring at the camera, Big John offered, "All you have to do is pick me up and slam me. It's all up to you, Andre. And remember if you don't do it you're retiring from the ring!"

Curtains for the Giant?

It was fight time, and Big John entered the ring first. To the now-familiar boos, he brandished the money-laden duffle bag while laughing at the crowd.

Andre the Giant began lumbering up the ramp. Being a wrestler for the past eighteen years brings with it a large following. The 475-pound Giant entered the ring to rousing applause.

Before the match began, the referee took the duffle bag from a reluctant Big John Studd. For safekeeping from "all those hungry people out there" the bag was held at ringside by a security guard.

Short and Sweet

The match began, and Big John scissored the Giant to the mat. Studd threw himself on the Giant. Appearing totally calm, the Giant

Andre the Giant beams after slamming Big John Studd to win the $15,000 challenge bout.

shrugged his massive shoulders, and Big John flew off.

The crowd sensed that this might be a short contest. They began taking up the chant, "Slam...slam...slam." Nodding in agreement, the Giant grabbed a charging Big John.

Andre tightened his arms around Studd, gripping him in a bear hug. Then with the crowd still cheering for the slam, Andre reached between Studd's legs and lifted him up.

Like a true showman, Andre still holding Studd turned to face directly the closed-circuit television cameras. Smiling, Andre slammed the struggling Studd to the mat.

With the crowd roaring, the referee awarded the Giant the money-filled duffle bag. Like a true gentleman, Andre took out some of the cash and threw it to the delirious ringside fans.

But, not one to lose graciously, Studd sneaked up on the Giant, snatched the bag away, and headed for the dressing room. The crowd laughed as Andre shrugged and waved good-bye.

WWF Tag-Team Championship —Windham/Rotundo vs. Volkoff/The Iron Sheik

A classic confrontation. A pair of American heroes against a Russian and an Iranian. The American tag team of Barry Windham and Mike Rotundo was managed by the irrepressible Captain Lou Albano. The foreigners, Nikolai Volkoff and the Iron Sheik, were under the supervision of Freddie "Ayatollah" Blassie.

Prior to the match, both managers were interviewed by Regis Philbin. Captain Lou looked almost clean-cut. His beard was gone, and his hair was trimmed. Maybe he really was taking his PEG (politeness, etiquette, grooming) to heart! When asked about his new look, the Captain responded, "I came clean for a movie. Aaron Russo, the director who made *The Rose*, asked me to shave the beard. I'm in a new picture with Danny DeVito and Joe Piscopo. Not a bad look for a fat guy of fifty-two years?"

Caught backstage at the Garden, a cane-wielding Freddie Blassie offered this to Regis: "I got the greatest tag team in the history of wrestling. I'm a star. I just finished a video for Cyndi Lauper. The whole thing was going down, falling on its face, who do they call on? Yours truly, me, Volkoff, and The Iron Sheik. Take that you pencil-necked geeks!"

Let the bout begin! The booing of the partisan crowd signaled the arrival of Blassie's team, the Iron Sheik and Nikolai Volkoff. As is their custom (or costume) Nikolai arrived wearing a T-shirt with the Russian hammer-and-sickle motif and carrying the Russian flag. The Iron Sheik came dressed in his Teheran finest and carrying the Iranian flag. Both wrestlers entered the ring to the fans' derisive catcalls.

Volkoff grabbed the microphone and proceeded to sing the Russian national anthem as the trio stood at attention. The crowd responded with chants of "USA! USA!" as many threw fruit, programs, and garbage into the ring.

After Volkoff's less-than-thrilling aria, the eyes of the crowd focused on the runway awaiting the appearance of Windham and Rotundo. They didn't have to wait long. As Bruce Springsteen's "Born in the U.S.A." played over the garden's sound system, Barry Windham and Mike Rotundo ran into the ring.

The Americans brought forth a standing ovation as the crowd sang along with Springsteen and clapped hands.

The referee checked both teams for foreign objects, forced the managers to leave the ring, and the match began. It didn't last long.

Windham, in the ring first for the Americans, took quick advantage of the Iron Sheik.

With a series of forearm smashes and tosses into the turnbuckle, Windham softened up the Sheik. Quickly, Windham retreated to his corner and tagged his partner, Mike Rotundo. Rotundo bounded into the ring before the Sheik could be relieved by Volkoff.

Rotundo pulled the Iron Sheik to the center of the ring before landing on him with an elbow to the windpipe. That was too much for Volkoff, who entered the ring and cracked his linked hands across the back of Rotundo's neck.

Windham then jumped into the ring to relieve Rotundo. As the referee was busy getting Rotundo and Volkoff out of the ring, his back was turned on Blassie.

As the crowd roared in anger, Blassie brought his wooden cane crashing down on Barry Windham's head. Windham collapsed, and the Sheik jumped on top to go for the pin.

A short three seconds later the referee awarded the World Wrestling Federation Tag-Team Championship to Nikolai Volkoff and the Iron Shiek.

Wendi Richter vs. Lelani Kai

This match was really a return engagement between Cyndi Lauper and the Fabulous Moolah. Cyndi, serving as Richter's manager, wanted to

Cyndi and Wendi get the crowd's attention just prior to the match with Lelani Kai.

get the championship title back from Lelani Kai, who was managed by the Fabulous Moolah and who had wrested the women's title away from Wendi.

Moolah and Kai entered the ring first, as villains are supposed to do. They didn't have to wait too long for their opponents.

As Lauper's "Girls Just Wanna Have Fun" boomed out of the loudspeakers, Richter and Cyndi danced their way into the ring. As they had done with the Springsteen song, the crowd sang along with Lauper and clapped hands.

To get the audience going Cyndi waved her arms, gesturing for the crowd to get into the music. Everybody, on their feet, sang along until the song concluded.

The most exciting thing about this match was the confrontation between Lauper and Moolah. Even as the referee was checking Richter and Kai for illegal objects prior to the opening bell, Cyndi and Moolah were nose to nose yelling at each other.

Eventually the referee started the match. For some reason, the women's events always turn into hair-pulling contests, and this one was no exception. Lelani Kai used Wendi's hair to toss her into a turnbuckle. Minutes later, Richter returned the favor by grabbing Kai's tresses and flipping her into the center of the ring.

Lelani Kai pulls on Wendi Richter's hair as the referee issues a warning.

Meanwhile, the crowd was busy watching the action outside the ring. The two managers, Moolah and Lauper, had maneuvered to the same side of the ring. The closer they got, the less the crowd paid attention to the action in the ring.

At one point, Lauper and Moolah were shoving each other as they screamed. In the ring, Kai had taken control, at least for the moment. Lelani delivered a flying drop-kick that drove Wendi into Kai's corner.

Moolah reached between the ropes and held Wendi's legs as Kai beat her with forearm smashes. In retaliation, Cyndi ran behind the Fabulous Moolah and, as the crowd roared with delight, smashed her over the head.

Moolah and Lauper wrestled to the ground. Eventually security guards pulled them apart. Now back at their respective sides of the ring, Lauper and Moolah continued to shout and point at each other.

Back in the ring, Wendi had made a turnaround. She grabbed Lelani Kai and slammed her to the mat. As the crowd cheered, she rolled Kai on her shoulders, administering a quick pin.

The World Wrestling Federation had a new women's champion in Wendi Richter. Then, as the Garden's loudspeakers played "Girls Just

Cyndi thumbs her nose at the vanquished Lelani Kai and her manager, the Fabulous Moolah.

Wanna Have Fun," Cyndi and Richter linked arms in the ring and danced in circles. Moolah and Kai argued with the referee, much to no avail.

The Garden party rocked and rolled as Cyndi and Wendi celebrated winning the title.

The Brawl to Settle It All

The bell at ringside rang slowly ten times. The crowd grew silent. After two hours of preliminary bouts, this was it. Referred to as anything from "The Grapple in the Apple" to "The Brawl to Settle It All," this, ladies and gentlemen, was the main event: Hulk Hogan and Mr. T trying for revenge against Rowdy Roddy Piper and Paul "Mr. Wonderful" Orndorff.

The Big Build Up

Before the combatants made their appearance, the Garden crowd was introduced to a few additional, and very special features. First of all, the guest ring announcer: Walking up the runway, dressed in a tuxedo with bright red cummerbund, was the former manager of the New York Yankees, Billy Martin. As Martin took the microphone, the audience gave him a standing ovation. After all, this was going to be a brawl, and who was more qualified to announce the festivities than Battling Billy!

Music legend Liberace joins the Rockettes as they entertain the Wrestlemania crowd. Later, he served as the guest timekeeper for "The Brawl to End It All."

Muhammad Ali, guest referee, smiles at one of his many admirers. Later, Ali brought the crowd to their feet as he mixed it up with Rowdy Roddy.

Of course no wrestling bout can exist without a referee. As the fans searched the runway, Billy Martin announced, "And now, ladies and gentlemen, your referee for today's main event, three-time former heavyweight champion of the world...a man who fought many great fights right here at Madison Square Garden — Muhammad Ali."

The delirious crowd welcomed their champ with an ear-splitting chant of "Ali...Ali...Ali!" Muhammad stepped between the ropes and entered the ring. After waving hello, he quickly threw a left-right combination as he shadow-boxed around the ring.

Billy Martin allowed the crowd to pay homage to Ali. Muhammad walked over to Billy and, as the photographers clicked away, playfully "tagged" Martin with a right to the chin.

Martin continued his role as announcer. "And now, if I can have your attentionn, please ...I'd like to introduce your guest timekeeper, a man who just set a world record for the quickest concert sellout of the New York Radio City Music Hall. Ladies and gentlemen — Liberace!"

Sure enough, dressed in a sequined shirt, Liberace strolled to ringside. Before he entered the ring, though, he gestured to the dressing room area. The crowd roared as four of the Rockettes, wearing bright red, feathered costumes, danced down the runway towards Liberace. Then they made their grand appearance in the ring. Liberace shimmied between the high-kicking chorus line. Again, another standing ovation. The Garden was rocking with excitement as everyone anticipated what was coming up next.

Bring on the Villains

Floodlights hit the dressing room entrance. The sound of bagpipes brought boos and catcalls from the audience. The curtains parted and twenty bagpipe players emerged in formation, dressed in traditional Scottish kilts. To the crowd, kilts and bagpipes could only mean one thing—Rowdy Roddy Piper!

Trailing his clansmen, Piper, grinning wildly, stepped onto the runway to begin his strut to the ring. Ignoring the booing crowd, Rowdy Roddy was having a grand old time. He seemed to appreciate being an important participant in the biggest thing ever to happen to professional wrestling. He exuded confidence.

Speaking to ABC's New York *Morning Show* host Regis Philbin just prior to the bout, Piper said, "I feel great. I'm in the pink. Look at me. Of course I'm confident. I'm not supposed to walk into a fight with tears in my eyes, for crying out loud. When you fight as much as I do, you get hurt once in a while."

Roddy Piper arrogantly smiles at a heckler during the introductions. Guest ring announcer Billy Martin approaches the microphone.

Philbin asked Piper about his chances of winning. "Of course I'm predicting victory," Piper chortled. "This is the biggest event ever to happen to this sport. Mr. T and Hulk Hogan, a movie star and a beach bum, should that scare me?. . .I think not!"

Accompanying Piper into the ring was his tag-team partner, Paul "Mr. Wonderful" Orndorff. If Orndorff's name sounds familiar, it should. A former professional football player with the Kansas City Chiefs, "Mr. Wonderful" turned to wrestling in 1978.

After waving to the booing crowd, Piper and Orndorff smugly awaited the arrival of their opponents.

The Tag-Team Titans

Again the floodlights hit the dressing room curtain. The crowd, now standing, began a rhythmic clapping. And then it began. "Eye of the Tiger" at full volume boomed over the sound system. The curtain parted. And bounding down the aisle, wearing a red velvet robe, looking mean, lean, and hungry was the one and only Mr. T. At ringside, Mr. T bobbed and wove, seeming really pumped up.

The floodlights hit the curtain again as the music rocked the Garden. Jumping into the spotlight was the bronzed brawler, the founder

Kilt-clad Rowdy Roddy Piper and Paul "Mr. Wonderful" Orndorff stare down Mr. T as he enters the ring.

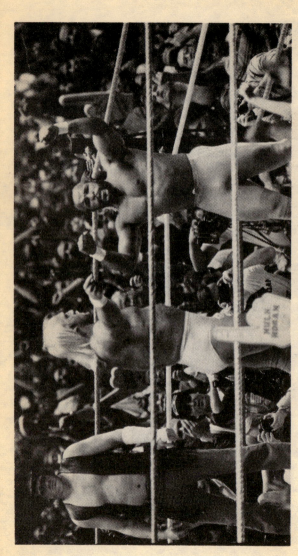

Hulk Hogan and Mr. T pump up before their match against Piper and Orndorff.

Prior to the match, the two tag teams mix it up in the ring.

and idol of the phenomenon known around the world as Hulkamania—Hulk Hogan!

Smiling, waving, and looking totally confident, the Hulkster strode over to Mr. T. They entered the ring together, confirming the strength of the partnership.

Mr. T removed his robe to display his tight Hulkamania T-shirt, identical to the one worn by Hogan. Hogan and T faced each other and stared, pumping up for the brawl. The Hulk tore his T-shirt off his body and threw it to the now wildly screaming crowd. As Mr. T nodded with approval, the Hulk reached over and tore Mr. T's shirt off!

It was almost time to get mean and nasty. Not to be ignored, Orndorff picked up a broom and took a swipe at Mr. T. Hulk Hogan quickly spun around and confronted Paul Orndorff. Piper jumped forward to meet the advancing Mr. T. The foursome pushed and shoved each other until broken up by ring security. The bell rang out, signaling ten seconds for Mr. T and Piper to go to their corners.

Let The Brawl Begin

Another bell rang. Hogan and Orndorff stood about four feet apart in the center of the ring. As Orndorff watched, the Hulk flexed his chest muscles, snarled, and motioned for Mr. Won-

Paul "Mr. Wonderful" Orndorff brandishes a broom handle toward the Hogan/Mr. T corner.

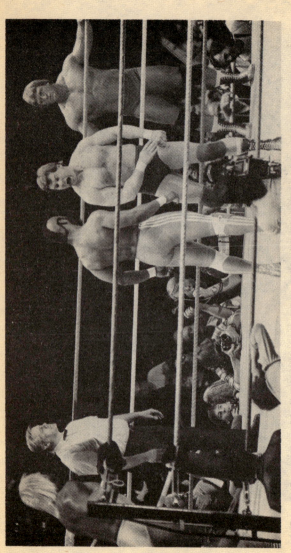

Rowdy Roddy slaps Mr. T as the match begins. A watchful Paul Orndorff gets ready to enter the ring.

derful to come closer. Before the first blow was even struck, Orndorff went back to his corner and slapped Piper's arm. The tag made, Piper replaced Orndorff in the ring.

Sensing that another change was in order, the Hulk looked around at the roaring crowd chanting, "T. . . .T. . . .T!" Nodding enthusiastically, Hogan strutted back to his corner. Slowly, graciously—almost regally—the Hulk lightly tapped Mr. T's outstretched hand. Mr. T eagerly hopped into the ring and rushed up to Piper.

Mr. T and the Rowdy One stood nose to nose. Piper slapped Mr. T on the side of the head. Now glaring, Mr. T returned the slap. Three more times they traded slaps, bringing roars from the frenzied crowd.

Piper grabbed Mr. T, pulled him into the ropes, and drop-kicked him to the mat. Pouncing on Mr. T, Piper drove his elbow into T's back. Mr. T writhed in pain as Piper repeatedly elbow chopped the back of his neck.

Hogan and Orndorff screamed, gesturing for their partners to mix it up. The roar from the fans was deafening. In the ring, Mr. T crawled away from Piper, trying to tag Hogan's waiting hand. Just inches before the tag could be made, Piper pulled T back to the center of the ring.

As the crowd, urged on by an irate Hulkster, cheered "T. . . .T. . . .T!" Mr. T rose up and

Mr. T lifts up Piper and spins him around. As the crowd cheered, Mr. T followed up the move by slamming Roddy to the canvas.

Hulk Hogan smashes the heads of Roddy Piper and Paul Orndorff together.

Mr. T and the Hulk team up ready to throw Roddy Piper across the ring.

Hogan jams Piper's feet into the canvas. Rowdy Roddy tries to ease the shock by holding on to the Hulk.

Mr. T controls Paul Orndorff as Hulk Hogan grabs hold of Roddy Piper. As the crowd roared, they smashed the Orndorff-Piper team in the middle of the ring.

surprised a charging Piper with a punch to the midsection. Piper doubled over in pain. Mr. T picked up Roddy, spun him around, and then to the delight of the crowd, slammed him onto the canvas.

Untagged, Orndorff illegally leaped into the ring and punched an unprepared Mr. T. Hogan rushed at Orndorff as Mr. T recovered. The foursome paired up, Hogan versus Orndorff, Mr. T versus Rowdy Roddy, as the free-for-all began. Body punches were exchanged. Security guards entered the ring trying to restore order to the match. They pulled apart the two pairs.

As he was being led back to his corner, Piper took a swipe at Muhammad Ali. Suddenly, the clock was turned back fifteen years, as Ali started boxing an astonished Piper, chasing him out of the ring. This was more than the crowd had ever dreamed of seeing. Chants of "Ali...Ali...Ali!" echoed through the arena.

In disgust, Piper and Orndorff left the ring and began walking back to the dressing room. The referee began to count them out, a count of ten meaning disqualification. The audience booed in disappointment at this early ending to the main event.

In order not to disappoint all those Hulkamaniacs, Hogan grabbed the referee's arms, stopping the count. The Hulk screamed to Piper and Mr. Wonderful, daring them to return.

Piper stopped in his tracks and led Orndorff as they stormed back to the ring. Mr. T returned to his corner, as Piper and Orndorff entered the ring. Hogan grabbed their heads and crashed them together. The crowd went crazy chanting "Hulk, Hulk!"

Hogan then kicked the bewildered Piper out of the ring. As the Hulk jumped down to continue the fight, Orndorff joined Rowdy Roddy as they teamed up to pummel Hogan. The referee tried to restrain an angry Mr. T. Finally, Mr. T just pushed the referee aside, flipped across the ring, and pulled Orndorff off the Hulk.

Hogan and Piper squared off in the middle of the ring. Piper picked up the Hulk and applied a backbreaker. Somehow Hogan escaped and tagged an eager Mr. T.

Mr. T rushed at Piper, but missed with a drop-kick. Flat on his back, Mr. T was "dead meat." And Piper "went for it." With a series of vicious kicks, Piper stomped Mr. T.

Arms lifted, Hogan urged the crowd to cheer on his partner. Hulkamania to the rescue! The roar of "T....T....T!" filled the Garden. Mr. T, obviously hurt, crawled over and tagged Hogan.

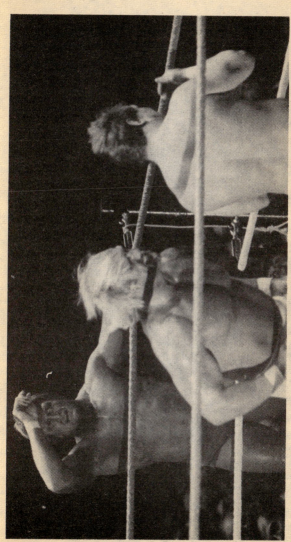

As Paul "Mr. Wonderful" Orndorff catches his breath, Hogan and Piper wage war in the ring.

Hogan applies a bear hug to Rowdy Roddy as Mr. T prepares to receive the tag.

Rowdy Roddy Piper leaps on Hulk Hogan's back. Seconds later, Hogan slammed Piper to the canvas.

Hogan applies a back slam to Paul "Mr. Wonderful" Orndorff.

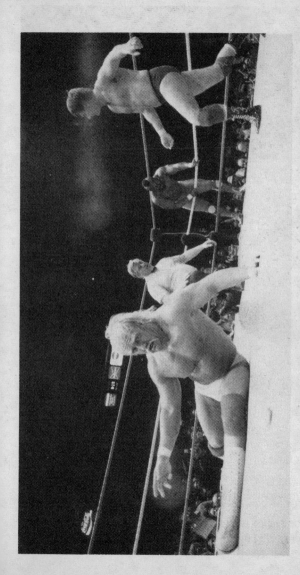

Mr. T enters the ring to prevent Piper from attacking Hulk Hogan.

Roddy Piper, assisted by Cowboy Bob Ornton, recovers
after getting thrown out of the ring. Muhammad Ali super-
vises the action.

The Hulk rushed into the ring, grabbed the obnoxious Piper, and pulled him over to Orndorff. Eyes glazed with anger, Hogan cracked their heads together again. Orndorff staggered to the center of the ring and collapsed. Hogan flew off the ropes, landing on Mr. Wonderful. A three-second count by the referee, and it was all over.

Hulkamania Forever

As Piper and Orndorff left the ring, Mr. T and the Hulk celebrated their well-earned revenge. Piper had paid dearly for the stomping of Cyndi Lauper and Captain Lou Albano.

As an exhausted Mr. T thanked Muhammed Ali, Billy Martin, Liberace, and the roaring crowd, the Hulk went into his victory pose, flexing his bodybuilder muscles.

"Eye of the Tiger" announced the end of the day's lineup. The elated crowd had witnessed the triumph of good over evil. Hulkamania lives.

Hulkamania and Beyond

In the future, it seems as if everybody will be touched by Hulkamania. Hulkamania as a media event is ready to skyrocket!

The fans of professional wrestling are

As Billy Martin watches, Hulk Hogan and Mr. T celebrate a hard-fought victory.

The body-flexing Hogan begins his famous victory dance.

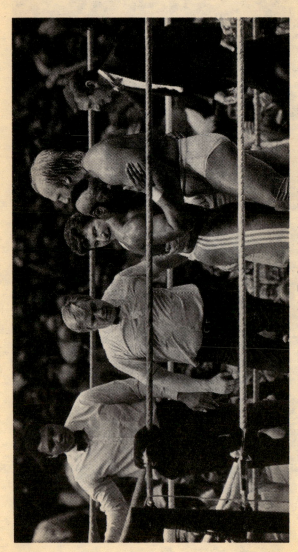

An exhausted Hogan grips Mr. T after winning their tag-team match.

clamoring for an opportunity to see the Hulk-ster at work. Hulk Hogan will most likely defend his World Wrestling Foundation title against the likes of Big John Studd and Nikolai Volkoff. There is also a rumoured rematch putting Mr. T and the Hulk against Rowdy Roddy Piper and Paul "Mr. Wonderful" Orndorff.

The Saturday morning television crowd will not be neglected, either. Coming in the late summer of 1985 an animated version of Hulk Hogan will star in a World Wrestling Federation cartoon show. Hulk will battle such animated nemeses as the Iron Sheik and Greg Valentine.

Once you have a cartoon it's a sure bet that toys will soon fill the shelves as well. In the world of product marketing, the WWF has contracted LJN toys to produce four superstar dolls. These scale reproductions standing five and a half inches tall are modeled after Andre the Giant, Big John Studd, Jimmy "Superfly" Snuka and, of course, everybody's favorite wrestler, Hulk Hogan. LJN's marketing manager Liz Wardley told *Us* magazine, "At the annual toy fair [early 1985], businessmen lined up to see the dolls and get autographs from the wrestlers. . .Other wrestlers can't wait to have a doll based on them."

The current popularity of wrestling has not gone unnoticed by the burgeoning world of video cassettes. Appearing at a video store near you will be two cassettes containing various professional wrestling highlights, starring Hulk Hogan and his grappling contemporaries. "Wrestling Bloopers, Bleepers, Bleeps and Body Slams" will feature segments of some of the sport's most memorable moments.

The big video best-seller is expected to be a tape entitled "Hulkamania." As part of the advance promotion, Hulk Hogan appeared at New York's famous Sardi's restaurant. The video produced by Coliseum Video, contains tapes of Hogan's greatest bouts against such notables at Nikolai Volkoff, Big John Studd, and Roddy Piper. To introduce the tape, Hogan unveiled a lifesize cardboard reproduction of himself that will be displayed at the video store locales.

Hulk Hogan has transcended the world of wrestling. Hulkamania has become the entertainment event of the decade. In these troubled times, America has found its new idol. We now have a tangible example of the triumph of good over evil. Hulk Hogan is Hulkamania!

PHOTO CREDITS